First published in Great Britain in 2001
by Greenwater Publishing
A division of Crystalsight Limited

A CIP catalogue record for this book is available
from the British Library

ISBN 1 903267 04 8

Printed and bound in Great Britain by The Bath Press, Bath

Matt Holland FROM WEMBLEY TO MOSCOW
A Diary of a Tractor Boy

Matt Thanks
"Fletch", Dad the family archivist, family and friends, particularly Paula for looking after the family in my many absences, all my teammates, everyone at the club and most importantly the fans, our twelfth player.

GREENWATER
PUBLISHING

CONTENTS

Introduction

Matt Holland - Introduction

What an extraordinary year! Whenever I think back over the season I can't quite believe what we achieved as a club. For the previous three years we had been developing but no one ever thought we would go from an exciting win at Wembley to 10 months later qualifying for the UEFA cup.

For the purposes of this book Wembley is the starting point, but I would like to pay tribute to the efforts of all those at the club in the preceding years who weren't with us in 2000. Success like ours doesn't happen overnight, it takes lots of hard work over many years and to everybody who has contributed, thank you.

Wembley, though, was the start of a new and exciting period for the club. To win there in any competition is fantastic but to do it in emphatic style, in front of 30,000 loyal and passionate fans, for promotion into one of the biggest and toughest football leagues in the world is something else.

Were you there? Did you enjoy it? How did you react when Martijn Reuser finished the game in the final minute? It was a superb strike but he could have bumbled it in off his knees and shoulders for all I cared. Somehow it seemed right though that we should leave Division One with a wonderful goal. After all we had played some wonderful football throughout the year.

It was a great day in front of the Twin Towers, particularly for all the fans and families as well as all involved professionally with the club. Remember, the three years before had promised so much and yet yielded little. Three consecutive stumbles in the play-offs, three years of excitement that ultimately ended in disappointment. This time we needed to win and we needed to join the Premiership. I think everyone involved with the club, players, staff, management and fans knew that. It didn't put pressure on us, though, because we felt we were good enough and this was our time. And the way football has gone recently, it needed to be. Anyone remotely interested in the game would understand the financial problems facing the smaller clubs. They just can't compete financially with Manchester United or Arsenal, let alone the big European clubs, so it was vital that we joined the Premiership, and once there competed. Who would have guessed that we would do both? Honestly?

The day after Wembley I started thinking about the next season. I took the family - Paula, Jacob and Samuel - to Cyprus and enjoyed our holiday but I knew Wembley was just the beginning for the club. We were in the Premiership! The place to be. The trick was to stay there and I don't mind admitting our aim was to survive. This might not sound very ambitious but the promoted clubs struggled every year and usually went straight back down.

So we set ourselves the target of 40 points. Statistics told us that if we reached that then we should survive and hopefully, with the extra money from Sky TV, start to work our way up the table in following seasons. Chairman David Sheepshanks even stated that once we reached 40 points and safety, plans for the new North Stand would be implemented. Not only were we playing for professional pride but for a better stadium!

A stadium that will now see European action. Whatever happens in the UEFA Cup can't take anything away from the achievement of actually qualifying for it. If a couple of results had gone the other way we might even have been in the Champions League. Occasionally during the summer I have reflected on how close we actually got and the disappointment we felt at not quite making it. To actually be thinking like that demonstrates how well we did.

What else happened during the year? We completed the transfer of Martijn Reuser for the start of the Premiership season and also paid a club record £4 million for Hermann Hreidarsson. During the season we lost David Johnson to Nottingham Forest. He had played a vital part in our push for promotion and scored lots of goals for the club but the excellent form of Marcus Stewart meant that Johnson featured mainly as a substitute.

Our other gain was the support of many fans around the country who appreciated our determination to play good football. It is one of the finest accolades a club can have when supporters of other clubs applaud. Many times I heard people discussing how good it was that Ipswich were doing well. These weren't diehard fans of the club but were genuinely pleased that we were succeeding without spending extravagant sums of money. It is probably fair to say that we became a lot of people's 'second team' and I felt there was a general surge of goodwill towards the unglamorous team from the countryside of Suffolk.

For that we must thank the management team. George Burley has constantly reiterated the importance of a good passing game and even in the years where we missed out on promotion, he refused to panic or change his philosophy. We certainly reaped the rewards when we did make it into the Premiership. And we must thank the humour of the fans who travelled up and down the country to support us. Wherever we played there was a section of blue and white and to the best of my knowledge their behaviour was impeccable.

While doing the research for this book and selecting the photographs for it, I kept remembering things that had happened during the season and in my mind kept playing certain passages of play or goals. Sometimes a photo is all that is needed to relive a moment and as you read the book I hope you experience the same feelings of fun, excitement and satisfaction as I have.

Let's hope there are many more exciting moments to come this season.

Matt Holland

First Half

May 2000

First Half

Barnsley v Ipswich Town, Nationwide Division 1
Play off Final

29 May 2000 Wembley Nationwide Division

Monday | 29 May 2000

Barnsley 1 v 4 Ipswich Town

WEMBLEY: Nationwide Division 1: Playoff Final

Standing in the tunnel before the game I felt nervous but also calm because I really felt we were going to win the game. Still, before the match there was the walk-out through the avenue of fireworks and the crowd noise to contend with and I knew these would put me slightly on edge, particularly the fireworks. I had been warned about them by the former Ipswich player, David Gregory.

He had played in the play-offs for Colchester United and told me that when the fireworks had gone off next to him he had nearly jumped out of his skin. Even though I was prepared they still startled me, but so did the cheer from the crowd as we walked onto the pitch. Both teams were met by a wall of noise and looking around the ground, it was good to pick out my family. Each player got 10 complimentary tickets for the game and another 25 they could buy. Somehow I picked up the spares from rest of the team and ended up with 50 tickets!

As much as I enjoyed the preamble it felt good to actually get the game underway, even though it wasn't the best of starts for us.

1-0 down in the fifth minute seemed surreal because I still felt we would win. We were the better side and just needed to keep our composure.

The goal itself was a little unlucky as well. It was a great strike from about 30 yards by Craig Hignett but it bounced back off the bar, hit our goalkeeper Richard Wright and then bounced in. Technically it is an own goal but I felt sorry for Richard. There was little he could do about it but we needed him to be on his best form for the rest of the game. This may sound bizarre but fortunately we had gone a goal down in the semi-final so we all knew what was required, no heads dropped and we continued to play to our plan, and as if the score was 0-0.

Sadly we lost David Johnson in the 21st minute to injury. He had played superbly all season, scoring many goals and often at crucial times so losing him in the final when 1-0 down was a blow, but Richard Naylor came on and played the game of his life. Six minutes later Tony Mowbray headed us back level and the belief that the team had in themselves was justified. Our passing and movement were good and I felt we were gradually starting to take control of the game, and indeed should probably have gone in at half-time in the lead. Instead the rest had to endure the turning point of the match as Richard Wright conceded a penalty by bringing down Hignett. On reflection I

1
It was a great boost to look round Wembley and see it decked out in blue.

2
Organising the team just before kick-off.

3
Tony Mowbray celebrates scoring the equaliser.

Monday | 29 May 2000

IPSWICH TOWN

understand exactly how important this moment was to us. Richard saved the spot-kick from Barnard and Although we went into the dressing room 1-1, we

actually felt like winners - that save had given us all a huge boost and the positive effect was almost tangible as the manager started his talk.

It got even better in the second half as Richard Naylor and Marcus Stewart both scored to make it 3-1. Richard's was a clinical strike from a man in form and demonstrated how well he and Marcus had gelled since Johnson's substitution. It wasn't over though as Hignett brought Barnsley to within one goal with a successful penalty and just as our nerves were stretched taut like piano wire, Hristov got behind our defenders and had a close header on goal. How Richard saved it I will never know but it was absolutely crucial as there were only six minutes remaining. A very nerve-racking, tense six minutes until Martin Reuser scored our fourth.

The Premiership prize was ours and I must confess to being thrilled by walking up the famous steps and raising the trophy towards the sea of blue.

The celebrations continued back at the Suffolk Showground but I was so tired I left with Paula quite early. A wise decision as apparently Jim Magilton took control of the microphone and refused to let anyone interrupt his monologue!

It had been a tiring few days with the build-up, two days in a hotel in Windsor, missing my son Samuel's first birthday party and then the adrenaline of the match itself. Next season though they would all be like that - the challenge had changed from winning to surviving.

1

Fulfilment of a boyhood dream, lifting a trophy at Wembley.

2

Old men can jump! Mowbray proves it by heading the equaliser.

3

The four goalscorers, Naylor, Mowbray, Reuser and Stewart celebrate. The banner says it all really.

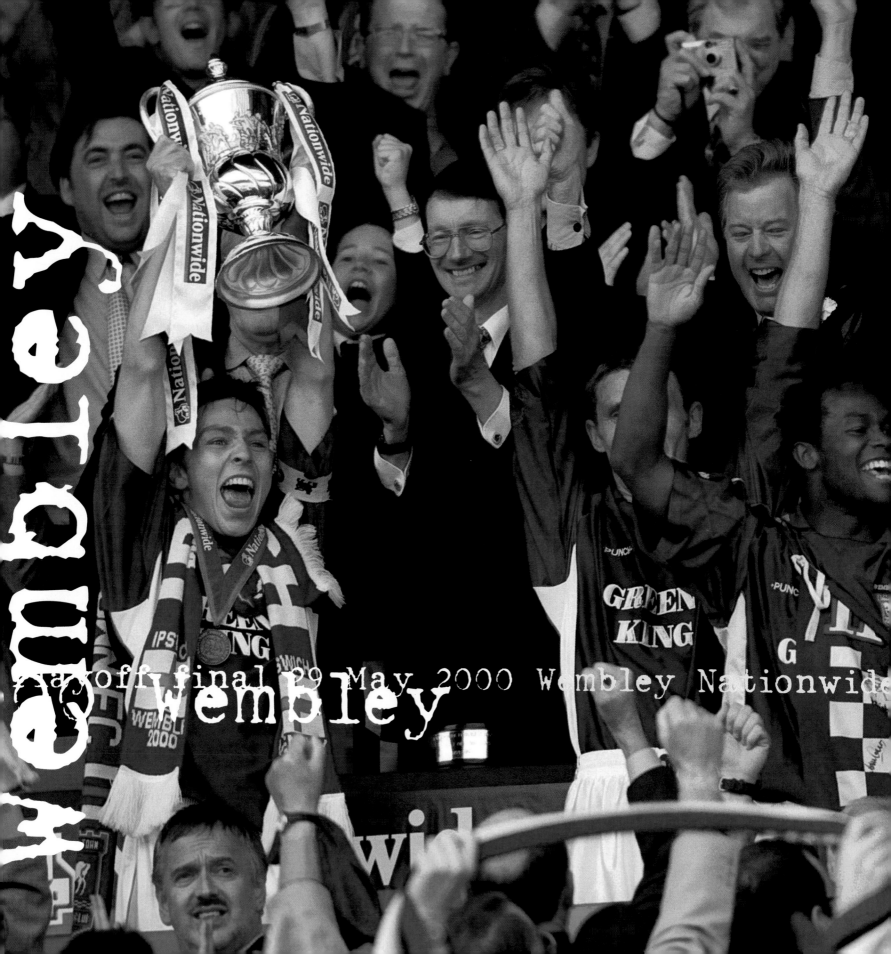

Wembley

Wembley

Play off final 29 May 2000 Wembley Nationwide

1

Basking in glory, the squad celebrate the end of a hard season.

August 2000

August 2000

Tottenham 3 - 1 Ipswich Town
Ipswich Town 1 - 1 Manchester United
Ipswich Town 1- 0 Sunderland

Saturday | 19 August 2000

Tottenham 3 v 1 Ipswich Town
White Hart Lane: FA Carling Premier League

When I first looked at the fixture list and saw Spurs away and Manchester United at home, I felt as if it was a bit 'Welcome to the Premiership'. Most people had us down for no points from a possible six, so it was important that we got something from these games, but the opener at White Hart Lane provided nothing other than the cachet of being the first Premiership team to score in the new season and a smidgeon of belief that we could actually compete at this level.

Mark Venus provided the goal and a dream start with a well-hit free kick but as much as I felt we were the better side, they were much more clinical in front of goal.

Our squad had been strengthened with the arrivals of Hermann Hreidarsson, John Scales and Martijn Reuser, who completed a move after being on loan to us at the end of the previous season, but we learned an important lesson immediately - possession has to be converted into chances and chances have to produce goals.

Pre-season had gone well. George Burley had reiterated his desire for us to prosper by playing attractive, passing football and, of course, we all had the fixed target of finishing anywhere above the bottom three clubs - the dreaded relegation zone. Recent history showed that the promoted clubs nearly always went straight back down, so survival was the ambition, and we felt 40 points would do it.

Ken Way, a sports psychologist, had a session with us all and he asked us what we expected and how many points we thought we'd get from the first three games?

I answered five points and I think the manager said nine. Ken's question to me was 'Why only five?'

Belief and a positive mental attitude were a must if we were to sustain acceptable performances throughout the whole season, so coming up against the biggest predator in British football, and one of the best sides in Europe was a massive test.

1

Mark Venus celebrates his goal.

2

First club to score in the Premiership, but it counted for nothing as we lost.

Tuesday | 22 August 2000

Ipswich Town 1 v 1 Manchester United

PORTMAN ROAD: FA Carling Premier League

Our first home game in the Premiership and against the undisputed best of Britain. What a fixture and what a result! We needed a confidence boost after the Spurs match and this sure provided it ...

We even took the lead in the sixth minute with a goal from Fabian Wilnis. David Beckham equalised in the 39th minute from a free kick that was a cross-cum-shot, but that was pretty much the end of the game for me. I touched the ball in front of Gary Neville on the left wing and he caught me late on my right ankle. Ironically, I had gone to the same school as Gary in Bury but had left aged nine when my dad's job moved down south. I don't really remember him because I was the year above but our parents know each other well, and after that tackle my ankle certainly knew him well.

It ended 1-1 and the dressing room was buzzing afterwards. We had played and held our own against the best and Sir Alex Ferguson even said that it was a good point for Manchester United - a huge compliment and very satisfying for the fans because the last time Ipswich had played Manchester United back in 1995, the result had been a humiliating 9-0 defeat.

Now we knew we could compete and all I needed to do was get fit for Saturday and Sunderland. Convinced of the healing powers of freezing-cold sea water, Burley sent me to the coast at Brightlingsea for treatment.

A worried Sir Alex Ferguson. A pleasant sight when you are the opposition.

A combination of Hreidarsson and Wright stop Manchester United's Andy Cole.

Saturday | 26 August 2000

Ipswich Town 1 v 0 Sunderland

PORTMAN ROAD: FA Carling Premier League

I had to undertake a fitness test at 11 a.m. and the physio strapped my ankle heavily and then made me complete sequences of twists, turns and headers to thoroughly test the stability of the ankle.

After 10 minutes Burley appeared and said:

'Can you pass with your right foot? Can you head it? GOOD. You're fit then.' And then he marched off.

His decisive attitude really helped me because it took any doubt out of my mind but I can't remember actually making a tackle during the game. I did work hard though and it was a fantastic feeling to be part of our first win.

Titus Bramble scored the goal in the 52nd minute and naturally received the plaudits but it was his defending that really impressed me. He closed down space, timed tackles perfectly and dominated so much at the back that Kevin Phillips was fairly innocuous.

When the final whistle went there was an almighty cheer - the fans obviously enjoyed the win as much as the players. It was a good follow-on from the United game and there was a definite purpose and belief in the team. We had four points out of a possible nine and felt we were surprising opposition teams.

My only problem was that my ankle swelled up and I had to miss the World Cup qualifier against Holland. I was very disappointed but the manager Mick McCarthy cheered me up by telling me I was in the squad for the game against Portugal, so instead of the delights of Amsterdam I went to Layer Road and watched Colchester United against my old club Bournemouth.

1

A pensive George Burley. The grey hairs prove he's the manager.

2

Our first win and Bramble is mobbed after the winning goal.

September 2000

September 2000

Leicester City 2 - 1 Ipswich Town
Ipswich Town 1 - 2 Aston Villa
Leeds United 1 - 2 Ipswich Town
Millwall 2 - 0 Ipswich Town
Ipswich Town 1 - 1 Arsenal
Ipswich Town 5 - 0 Millwall
Everton 0 - 3 Ipswich Town

Wednesday | 6 September 2000

Leicester City 2 v 1 Ipswich Town
FILBERT STREET: FA Carling Premier League

Since the injury against Manchester United I had been unable to train and it started to affect my performances. I was relying on basic gym work and the actual games to keep me going, but that is not enough and I was losing sharpness around the pitch. I particularly felt it in this match, which was our worst performance of the season. Both teams played three at the back; Scales making his debut for us so it was disappointing to concede both goals through defensive error. Burley really let us know what he thought after the match and with good reason. It was a poor-quality match and we gave a poor-quality performance. Good sides still manage to eke out points and results even when playing badly and if judged by that criteria we were far from being a good side. After the euphoria of the two previous results, this one came as a rude shock, although in the long run it probably woke us up to the threat of complacency.

IPSWICH TOWN

Saturday | 9 September 2000

Ipswich Town 1 v 2 Aston Villa

PORTMAN ROAD: FA Carling Premier League

Whenever I think of this match I see the horrific photo featured of Luc Nilis breaking his leg. He had played brilliantly in Euro 2000 for Belgium and a few months later he collides with another player and is forced to retire. Thankfully this is a rarity, but even so it is an ever-present danger for footballers. The game is played at great pace and some thumping tackles are made, and it only takes a moment of misjudgement for a serious injury to occur.

The plus side for Ipswich was the impact Marcus Stewart made when he came on. He had been dropped for the Leicester match and we were struggling to score goals because Stewart and David Johnson weren't combining well. Our scorers thus far had been mainly defenders - Bramble, Venus and Wilnis. We needed to start threatening from up front and this was the first game in which we did - and it all happened with Stewart coming on. His 90th-minute goal was not enough after Lee Hendrie (28th) and Dion Dublin (55th) had scored for Villa to earn them their first win, but it proved he had channelled his anger about being dropped into performing better. How much more we were to enjoy for the rest of the season but at this time we were happy he had scored, disappointed to lose and distraught for Luc Nilis.

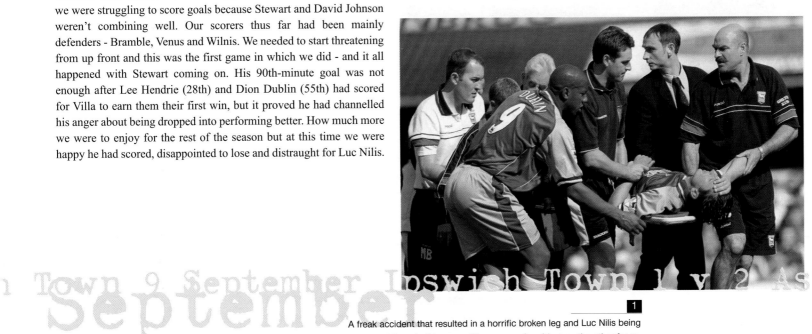

A freak accident that resulted in a horrific broken leg and Luc Nilis being stretchered off in agony. The concern is evident on the other faces.

Saturday | 16 September 2000

Leeds United 1 v 2 Ipswich Town
Elland Road: FA Carling Premier League

I had only started training again for a couple of sessions after a scan on the ankle but I felt better going into the game having trained comfortably, if not necessarily all that well. The fact that I was back in the routine of work made me feel comfortable and I was determined to improve on my last two games. Neither were ones to look back on and cherish and I am convinced that being unable to train was responsible. That is not an excuse - I never look for nor believe in them - but a realistic analysis of my play before, during and after the injury.

Leeds had suffered a lot of injuries to their squad and been thrashed 4-0 in the Nou Camp by Barcelona during the week. We felt they would be affected but were still aware that they were fielding ten players with international experience at some level. They played 4-3-3 and we went 4-4-2: Jim Magilton, Jamie Clapham, Jermaine Wright and myself in midfield to try and dominate from the centre. It was a bad start as Lee Bowyer scored in the 4th minute but James Scowcroft equalised in the 12th and slowly we started to control the midfield. The report in the Yorkshire Post said that Magilton and I were outstanding in midfield, and being a Lancashire lad I really enjoyed that compliment from a Yorkshire newspaper. The winning goal by Jermaine after a one-two with Stewart close to the goal was exquisite, both in build-up and execution as he neatly clipped it past goalkeeper Nigel Martyn.

It was the ideal start to the second half and ultimately brought our second win of the season and, importantly, our first away win. It felt good to be winning again and personally I thought it had been my best match of the year. I particularly enjoyed a hard but fair tackle on Oliver Dacourt in about the 60th minute. The night before in the hotel I had listened to him being interviewed on TV and when asked what he thought of Matt Holland he replied that he didn't know me.

There was a definite edge to our performance. We had more bite, I certainly did and the result was justified. It was just what we needed after two poor games and started a good run of games in the league. We weren't getting flustered if we conceded a goal and were starting to construct attacking moves and openings for the front players.

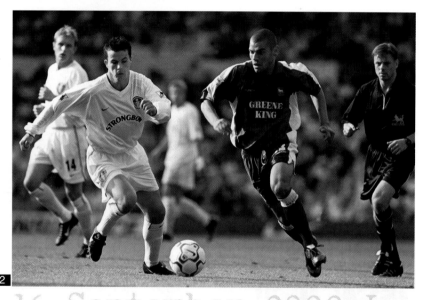

1
Stewart congratulates Wright on his winner against Leeds.

2
Jermaine Wright - runs past Ian Harte.

3
Jermaine Wright celebrate's scoring.

Tuesday | 19 September 2000

Millwall 2 v 0 Ipswich Town
THE DEN: Worthington Cup Second round 1st Leg

I sat out the first half, which was annoying for two reasons. First, I hate not playing. Whatever the game and whatever the prize, I would rather be on the pitch, trying something to get the result. Second, I am a dreadful watcher of games. On the bench or in the stands I kick every ball and make every tackle. Even at home on the sofa I can't help myself fidgeting about. I had spoken to the physio, Dave Williams, on the Sunday and told him that my ankle felt better than in the previous few weeks but he told me that Burley was going to rest me. I argued, but to no avail. I sat on the bench for the first time for the club in a competitive match.

We went 1-0 down in the 37th minute which wasn't surprising considering how poorly we played. Millwall were managerless and yet they played like a club with a purpose, while we were supposedly performing well in the Premiership and yet played as if we'd only just met each other. I came on at half-time for Reuser and Wilnis came on for Croft but the team didn't improve much, if at all. We conceded another goal in the 80th minute and waited for the manager to say his piece. The original plan had been to play 5-3-2 but it didn't work so it was soon switched to the more conventional 4-4-2. That didn't do much better and quite rightly Burley went mad in the dressing room afterwards - we deserved it. He described it as our worst performance and tore into Jermaine Wright, accusing him of believing his own press after the Leeds game. In three days he had gone from hero to villain - it really is a thin line that separates the twin impostors, success and failure. We had a lot to do in the second leg if we were to stay in the Worthington Cup, which like many middle-ranking sides we viewed as an excellent route into Europe.

1
Losing to Millwall hurt the manager and he certainly let us know it in the dressing room afterwards.

2
Me and Millwall's Tim Cahill go up for the header.

Saturday | 23 September 2000

Ipswich Town 1 v 1 Arsenal
PORTMAN ROAD: FA Carling Premier League

1
Marcus Stewart celebrates his goal.

2
Despairing dive could not prevent Dennis Bergkamp's equaliser.

3
Passing the baton. Arsenal's old and new keepers shake hands.

Managers have a difficult job. Everyone knows that, although at the same time everyone also thinks they can do better. After the Millwall defeat Burley had to ensure we were prepared for Arsenal. We were certainly motivated - the loss to Millwall had shocked us but we also knew we had to be on top form for the Gunners. Jermaine showed his determined character by playing brilliantly. A week ago he had scored the winner against Leeds and played superbly. Then came Millwall and a personal roasting by the manager. To accept that, work extra hard in training and then produce a man-of-the-match performance against a side as good as Arsenal proves how mentally tough and resilient Jermaine is.

We took the lead in the 49th minute after I crossed for Stewart and I really felt we were going to win the game. Stewart was a real handful up front for them and Titus Bramble defended astutely and powerfully against Thierry Henry ... Annoyingly, Denis Bergkamp equalised with only six minutes to go.

Later that night Paula and I went to a friend's for dinner and we all ended up watching the game on Match of the Day. I felt frustrated that we hadn't won but pleased with our performance, especially the players I have already mentioned.

I rarely sleep after a game and often lie awake until 3 or 4 a.m. replaying moments of the game in my mind and working out how we could have played better. All I could think of after this match as I stared at the ceiling was a header I had missed that should have won the game. Burley had also said straight after the match that I should have been closer to Kanu for their goal and when I saw it on Match of the Day I agreed.

Another sleepless night but as dawn broke I realised that for a team supposedly destined for relegation we had taken five points off three Champions League teams - Manchester United, Leeds United and Arsenal. It all counted for nothing though when Jacob and Sam jumped on the bed demanding breakfast. One day I'll explain to them how annoyed I was at missing that header!

Tuesday | 26 September 2000

Ipswich Town 5 v 0 Millwall

PORTMAN ROAD:Worthington Cup Second round 2nd leg

Phew! A close-run thing, even though the scoreline suggests otherwise.

We needed two goals to push it into extra time and we didn't get them until they had their second player sent off in the 73rd minute.

The first had been sent off in the 29th, but Jim Magilton had missed the penalty and for all our advantage of being one man up for the next 50 minutes, we still couldn't score. Johnson in the 74th and Bramble in the 87th duly delivered the necessary scores and extra time was ours with a two-man advantage, superior fitness and injuries to two more of their players. They had used all their substitutes and two of their players just sat down on the touchline but the referee had to call them back on the pitch.

I scored in the 91st, my first goal of the season and fiftieth career goal.

Through to the next round, although not without scares but we were delighted to keep all routes to Europe open.

Saturday | 30 September 2000

Everton 0 v 3 Ipswich

GOODISON PARK: FA Carling Premier League

Before the match my instructions were to man-mark Gazza.

For all the problems - self-inflicted or otherwise - he has experienced in his career, he could still play a superb game and we wanted to shut him out. It was definitely different playing against him. He talked non-stop throughout the game, a lot of it being very humourous. Also, he had 'HOLLAND 8' written on his hand. I asked him why and he grinned: 'So I remember who I'm supposed to be marking.' He played quite well but Everton were poor and no match for us.

John McGreal scored our first in the 19th minute - which he took great pleasure in as he is a Liverpool fan - and then Stewart finished them off with two well-taken goals.

He was continuing his good form which augured well for the next few matches and there is a correlation between him playing well in this period and the team having their best spell of the season.

The manager kept reminding us that to make any mark in the league we needed a succession of good results. The odd win would possibly be enough for survival, but we were now convinced we were better than that.

The Everton fans certainly thought so because they gave us a standing ovation after the game. A fan can give no greater compliment to the opposing team.

With the manner of the win fresh in my mind, I was in good spirits as I joined the Republic of Ireland squad for the crucial match away to Portugal.

1

One to One. I'm supposed to be man-marking Gazza, so, where am I.

2

At least I can find Marcus and help him celebrate one of his two goals that defeated Everton.

October 2000

October 2000

Portugal 1 - 1 Republic of Ireland
Republic of Ireland 2 - 0 Estonia
Ipswich Town 1 - 1 West Ham
Bradford City 0 - 2 Ipswich Town
Ipswich Town 2 - 1 Middlesbrough

Saturday | 7 October 2000

Portugal 1 v 1 Republic of Ireland

FIFA World Cup European Qualifying Group 2

The team was announced on Wednesday and I was on the bench. This is always disappointing but international football is a squad game and it's better to be part of a squad than not. We had been disappointed with the draw with Holland because we felt we could have won it, so there was a steely resolve about the squad as we assembled. Portugal are an exceptional side and we wanted a point from this match.

The first half was goalless and five minutes before the break, Mick McCarthy told me that I was on for the second half to sit in front of the back four and allow Roy Keane and Mark Kinsella to get forward.

Whatever match, important World Cup qualifier or friendly, I love getting on the pitch and I spent the half-time break watching the clock tick slowly round. We had been under pressure for a lot of the first half and it resumed immediately when play started again. Something had to give and in the 56th minute it did - Sérgio Conceição cutting in from the right to score.

It was with the run of play really and nothing more than they deserved, but rather than panic, we settled into a pattern of play - a pattern that gave me my most memorable moment on a football field yet.

The ball was worked down the right flank and Stephen Carr passed it infield to me. Instinctively, I looked to pass or whip a cross in but no one came to close me down so I pushed forward for about five yards. The Portuguese defence seemed reluctant to pressure me although none of my teammates seemed able to get free to receive the ball. I carried it another five yards and then hit it. I was 25 yards from goal, there were only 14 minutes left and we were losing 1-0. I knew I'd hit it well and everything went into slow motion as I watched it squeeze between the outstretched hand of the diving goalkeeper and the post - my first international goal! I can't remember what I did next and even when I watch it on TV I never see the celebrations, just the ball going in.

The point we wanted was ours if we could defend for 14 minutes and I had earned it. I so desperately wanted it to count for something and I had the opportunity to ensure it did by man-marking Luis Figo, the then most expensive footballer in the world, for the last ten. I didn't know before how strong he is on the ball. Most people talk about him and Zinedane Zidane and their skills and excellence, but without strength they would get bustled off the ball. Luckily the game fizzled out and we got the draw. The team went mad in the dressing room afterwards but before getting there. I had to endure a giant hug from the manager! Like me he was ecstatic and joked about me being too far forward for the job I was supposed to be doing. He even said it to the press: 'Of course I told Matty to stay back and I've had a joke with him that I don't want him getting forward like that again!'

Leaving the dressing room I was mobbed by a melee of press and cameras and they shouted questions at me as flashlights kept dazzling my eyes. I was on a massive high and the team celebrated throughout the night. When I got to bed I read through the congratulatory messages on my mobile phone from the Ipswich boys, and an indecipherable one from my brother Martin, who must have been very drunk indeed.

What a night!

Wednesday | 11 October 2000

Republic of Ireland 2 v 1 Estonia

FIFA World Cup European Qualifying Group 2

Back on the bench!

There was still a very important job to do after the draw on Saturday and at home, this was a must-win game if we were to compete in the group with Portugal and Holland. We played 4-4-2 with the same starting eleven as the Portugal game and played well. It was a comfortable win but I didn't get on which was disappointing because I still hadn't made my home debut at Lansdowne Road. Our autumn series of World Cup qualifiers had gone very well with five points and draws against the two major nations, Holland and Portugal. March was the next game so domestic football dominated again and I was at least going back to a winning team with a great spirit.

Saturday | 14 October 2000

Ipswich Town 1 v 1 West Ham
PORTMAN ROAD: FA Carling Premier League

A visit from my first club.

I had joined West Ham from school after Frank Lampard Sr had spotted me and it was good to meet up with him again. Who knows? Without him I might be doing something completely different. I had enjoyed five years with The Hammers before moving to Bournemouth and I hardly knew any of the players. The turnover of staff at professional clubs is astonishing. The kit manager was the same though. Eddie Gilhem had been a friend when I was there and he gave me Igor Stimac's shirt which I passed on to Ron, one of the stewards at Portman Road.

Annoyingly, we didn't win the game despite Stewart scoring in the fifth minute from a Wilnis cross and then dominating the rest of the half. Magilton hit the post, we camped in their half and yet failed to turn our advantage into goals and, finally, we suffered for it when Paulo di Canio snatched an equaliser in the 72nd minute. How could I complain? I had done the same thing against Portugal, but we should've won. Instead of three points I picked up bruises as they kicked me black and blue. Maybe they were gestures of affection for an old player.

1 Igor Stimac and I would be useless at 'Spot the Ball' but win a gurning competition.

2 I finished the game covered in bruises and it's not hard to see why?

3 Me and West Ham's Joe Cole in action.

Saturday | 21 October 2000

Bradford City 0 v 2 Ipswich Town

VALLEY PARADE: FA Carling Premier League

Negotiations about a new contract had been ongoing since the start of the season and on the Friday the final issues had been resolved and I signed. I had always wanted to but there were a few sticking points; both for the club as well as me, but thankfully both parties were very satisfied with the final deal. What I needed now was a good performance to maintain the personal momentum I had developed.

Bradford were the perfect opponents because they were a must-win fixture for us and I was buzzing before the game started. The pre-match talk by Burley had concentrated on us continuing to play good football. If we did that he felt the wins would keep coming. Burley had a lot of confidence in his team and it rubbed off on the players. Our away form had been good and Bradford were struggling - three points were ours if we maintained our standards.

Like so many games before we played beautifully but failed to kill off the opposition. We took the lead from a Dan Petrescu own goal in the 33rd minute. I tried to whip in a cross from the left between the goalkeeper and the defender and his defensive lunge finished as clinically as any striker could have. But it took us until the 87th minute to score the second, a Clapham free kick. Despite our excellent run of good results and our position near the top of the table, we weren't ruthless enough.

I was still mulling this over the next day when I read in the News of the World that my new contract was worth £20,000 a week. I was with Paula at a riding event and unbeknown to me, Jacob, my eldest son, had read this but with the timing that only kids and animals have, waited for some of our friends to be present before proudly announcing: 'My dad earns £20,000 a week.'

Embarrassed, I explained that I didn't but all they did was laugh and insist on me buying the drinks. For the rest of the day Jacob's mouth was kept busy by a never-ending supply of sweets!

1. Relieved when Jamie Clapham scored our second goal against Bradford, we celebrated with a group hug.

2. I felt I was getting back to form after the injury and just beat Dan Petrescu to this ball.

3. Not the time to talk to us about insurance and pensions.

Saturday | 28 October 2000

Ipswich Town 2 v 1 Middlesborough

PORTMAN ROAD: FA Carling Premier League

There were great vibes around the club at this time and there is no doubt in my mind as to what was causing it - results.

Our supporters - home and away - were deafening. The pass-and-play football we were playing was not only effective but attractive, and we were hanging around the top five and six of the Premiership. But still people were referring to us as relegation fodder. They were blind to the quality of the football we were playing and the intense passion and desire that George Burley had fostered. We weren't there to be cannon fodder for the so-called big clubs. I'll accept we may have been punching above our weight but the belief through the club was that we would soon deserve a re-rating and people would have to start taking us seriously.

This game was a perfect example. Middlesborough had big money, big ambitions and big problems. Admittedly, they were without Alen Boksic and Paul Ince but on the field we could sense their lack of confidence; it was almost tangible in their mannerisms and play. I hit a post early on but we went 2-0 up through goals from Richard Naylor and Mark Venus, which was no more than we deserved.

We were sharp and enjoying games. Really it was just an extension of the training ground and the hard work everyone was putting in there. Sessions were fun, football was fun and the results were most definitely fun. Despite the good result I felt sorry for their manager Bryan Robson because he had been my childhood hero. I even saw him at the end of the season on holiday in Marbella but I was too nervous to go up and speak to him!

I was very proud, however, to have a Daily Telegraph 'Scouting Report' piece done on me by former Arsenal striker Alan Smith. So much of what he wrote was similar to the manner of Robson's play - even we players have heroes, not necessarily in the same sport, but we have them all the same.

1
We keep celebrating.

2
Richard Naylor earning his nickname 'Psycho' against Middlesbrough.

The Daily Telegraph Scouting Report by Alan Smith

ON THE face of it, there would appear to be something quite special going on at Ipswich Town. Fifth in the table after Saturday's well-deserved victory over Middlesborough, the Premiership new boys are off to an unexpected flyer.

There's no great secret to this early success unless, that is, you count a swift passing game in which everyone knows their place together with the importance of working hard for each other. At the very heart of this efficient system sits Matt Holland. A conscientious, amazingly energetic player, there aren't many who come remotely close if we're talking sheer dependability.

An ever-present since his debut three years ago, Ipswich's captain was making his 180th consecutive appearance at the weekend. And that from a central midfield position requiring uncompromising commitment to the cause.

Somewhere along the line you would expect Holland to have picked up a knock that needed tender loving care. Apparently not. The closest he came was against Millwall this season in the Worthington Cup. Starting on the bench, only half the match had elapsed before he was back in the thick of the action.

There isn't a coach in the world - not even Sven Goran Eriksson - who can forcibly instill that kind of hunger and enthusiasm. It came originally from watching Bryan Robson as a boy. Holland's regular trips to Old Trafford persuaded him to try to emulate Robson's awe-inspiring performances. Now, as manager of Middlesborough, Robson would surely have been impressed as Holland made run after run into the penalty area. Acting almost as a third striker, the midfielder got on the end of several crosses as Ipswich swept irresistibly forward.

His firm header from a Mark Venus corner thumped the bottom of the near post before a brave diving effort from Fabian Wilnis's swirling cross plonked straight into the midriff of a thankful Mark Crossley.

It's all very well latching on to such moves, a knack which requires perfect timing in itself, but you also need great lung capacity to funnel back afterwards. Holland can keep up with the best of them when it comes to running, easily gaining the upper hand over the lack-lustre Christian Karembeu in that vital middle area.

Confident enough to continue the forays forward, the skipper had a hand in Ipswich's opener. Racing on to a long through ball, he panicked Crossley into a hurried clearance that Richard Naylor gratefully snapped up.

With few fancy trimmings to his game, Holland often presents possession to the more creative Jim Magilton once the ball's been won. Nothing wrong with that. The Republic of Ireland player knows his limitations to the same degree he knows his strengths.

Roy Keane and Mark Kinsella restrict international appearances but a smartly-taken goal against Portugal recently showed he's well at ease in that company.

Not surprisingly therefore, the Premiership holds little fear either. While adopting a more restrained role in the second half, he still managed to connect with Naylor's knock-down for a volley which sailed too high. Moments later he was seen tidying up deep in his own half.

This small cameo sums up Holland's game. Always on the lookout in attack but ready to defend when it matters. It was from his foul on Noel Whelan that the visitors scored but the captain wasn't to be denied and led his side on to victory.

As if he had not covered enough ground already, Holland ran right round the pitch at the final whistle - something he does, win, lose or draw - to thank the Suffolk crowd. An honest, whole-hearted performer, Holland, it seems, just won't lie down.

Reproduced by courtesy of The Daily Telegraph.

November 2000

November 2000

Arsenal 1 - 2 Ipswich Town (Worthington Cup)
Newcastle United 2 - 1 Ipswich Town
Ipswich Town 2 - 0 Charlton Athletic
Republic of Ireland 3 - 0 Finland (Friendly)
Coventry City 0 - 1 Ipswich Town
Manchester United 2 - 3 Ipswich Town
Ipswich Town 2 - 1 Coventry City (Worthington Cup)

Wednesday | 1 November 2000

Arsenal 1 v 2 Ipswich Town

HIGHBURY: Worthington Cup 3 round

This was pretty much against a second-string Arsenal side full of youngsters. Still, a win at Highbury is always good and it did extend our unbeaten run to seven matches. Sylvan Wiltord was outstanding but we overpowered them in midfield and despite not playing particularly well, we did enough and still had three avenues leading to Europe.

IPSWICH TOWN

1

1

The Worthington Cup was a possible route to Europe for us whereas it seemed nothing more than an inconvenience for Arsenal

2

One minutes silence.

2

ARSENAL · 8 45:00
IPSWICH

1 November 2000 Arsenal 1 v 2 Ipswich Town

Saturday | 4 November 2000

Newcastle 2 v 1 Ipswich Town

ST JAMES PARK: FA Carling Premier League

'We'll meet again, don't know where, don't know when.' OK, I know the Vera Lynn tune from the Second World War doesn't quite fit because we did know where and we did know when, but the sentiment is apt because Kieron Dyer had been such an important and popular part of Ipswich Town.

It was my job to man-mark him and I felt I did a good job because he did little of note in the game. Ironically, though, he cleared a header of mine off the line, so I suppose our personal battle ended up evens.

We took the lead in the 13th minute by Stewart, not that my dad could tell. He was with the travelling Ipswich fans and they were all stuck up in a far corner of the stand. Alan Shearer

equalised in the 22nd minute and then won the game for them in the 67th with a dubious penalty, although it was hard for the referee not to give it in front of 50,000 Geordies. Mark Venus tackled Shearer in the box and from where I was the ball went sideways, suggesting that he got a touch. I saw the TV replays later and it did look more like a penalty on screen, but at the time I was bitterly disappointed that it was given. We had fought well and deserved a point but Shearer's awareness and canny nature had won the game and ended our unbeaten run.

I was then told after the match that Kevin Beattie, a former Ipswich Town player, had criticised my performance on Radio Suffolk. My primary job had been to keep Dyer quiet, which I had done, something the newspaper reporters at the match appreciated even if Beattie hadn't. When I was younger I would have queried the issue with Beattie himself but criticism is part of the job, and it is a job that we get well paid for. It has to be accepted in the same manner as praise. I knew I'd done well and so did my teammates, besides the result is always more important and we hadn't got that. Part of the problem, I think, was that we were starting to rely on Stewart to score all the goals. We had plenty of possession in the game and plenty of opportunities. Maybe we needed more input from midfield or more attacking nous and goals?

One difference I had noted since my goal against Portugal was the level of media interest in me. Before the Newcastle game I had done the Last Word show on Sky with Jimmy Hill, then a feature interview with the Independent on Sunday, a piece with Channel 5 and finally a slot on Sky's Soccer AM.

I must confess to enjoying the media side of being captain, particularly because a lot of media people are very knowledgeable about football. Jimmy Hill was excellent, thoughtful and possessed a good insight into the game. There is a lot of grumbling and moaning done by footballers about the media but I think we should embrace them. Simply put, without them the game would be a lot smaller. Every Thursday during the season is Press Day at Ipswich and I like to think that the club and its staff have a good relationship with all mediums of the press at both local and national level.

At least the feedback that I've had suggests we do.

1

Two months after winning triple-jump gold in the Sydney Olympics, Jonathon Edwards turned up to watch his home team Newcastle United.

2

A consistent feature of the season. The lads congratulating Stewart on another goal.

3

Shearer and I lead the sides out. By the end of the game his face had come back to haunt us.

4

To Blues and England fans he needs no introduction. Bobby Robson and George Burley are two of the best managers the club has ever had.

November

4 November 2000 Newcastle 2 v 1 Ipswich To

stle 2 v 1 Ipswich

Saturday | 11 November 2000

Ipswich Town 2 v 0 Charlton Athletic
PORTMAN ROAD: FA Carling Premier League

I scored my first Premiership goal, which was a relief because I had recently started worrying about the lack of goals from our midfield.

It was interesting to play against one of the other promoted sides and see how they were coping in the top league (pretty well it must be said). We dominated this match, although, again our inability to turn possession and territorial advantage into goals was frustrating.

I was beginning to wonder if this was going to be 'one of those days' when with ten minutes to go Hermann Hreidarsson passed to me, I shaped to shoot with my right foot but cut back inside my Republic of Ireland teammate Mark Kinsella and hit it. I was on the edge of the box on the left-hand side and it went in the left-hand side of the goal, much to my pleasure and to the relief of everyone in the team who had squandered numerous chances earlier in the match - including me.

Stewart - who else? - finished it off five minutes later and George Burley was very complimentary to me afterwards about my performance. He spent a lot of the post-match chat in the dressing room reiterating the importance of us keeping our work rates high throughout the whole match. He was pleased with the performance and the result, but he is such a good manager because he constantly analyses and seeks to improve.

I had to fly to Ireland for a friendly against Finland and my travelling companion was none other than Kinsella. Sitting next to each other we both read the papers reports of how I had fleeced him!

Mark is a great man and laughed about it, which was just as well because his mum and dad met us at the airport and drove us both to the hotel. Throughout the journey his dad ribbed him for allowing me past to get the goal, which was probably the last thing he needed.

1
An unsung hero. Alan Ferguson, our groundsman before the Charlton game.

2
Down I go against Charlton Athletic. Must have been a foul.

3
It cannot be fun getting wet but we truly appreciate your loyalty and support.

Wednesday | 15 November 2000

Republic of Ireland 3 v 0 Finland

FIFA World Cup European Qualifying Group 2

No way we could outwit each other in this match because we were paired alongside in central midfield. This was my first game at Lansdowne Road, a stadium full of passion - entirely due to the crowd. It was a fantastic feeling running out on to the pitch.

Steve Finnan, Steve Staunton and Kevin Kilbane scored the goals in what was a comfortable victory but I will always cherish my first game at the home stadium. Besides, it gave me first-hand experience of how good Jari Litmanen was. He moved to Liverpool later in the season and it was easy to see why Gerard Houllier thought so much of him.

I flew home elated and satisfied, looking forward to a weekend without a game because we were the featured match on Monday Night Football on Sky Sports.

Monday | 20 November 2000

Coventry City 0 v 1 Ipswich Town
HIGHFIELD ROAD: FA Carling Premier League

This was the Monday Night Football game on Sky and we were very keen to win and show the public that our success was based on the basic principles of good football, passing and retaining possession.

Annoyingly, the pitch was of a very poor standard, which prevented the game from being an enjoyable spectacle, but we did at least get three points. It was hard work though and it took an inspired moment by the substitute Martijn Reuser to get the goal. His energy from the moment he came on lifted us and it was from his cross in the 89th minute that Fabian Wilnis scored. Our desire to win was fully evident by the number of men we threw forward as the game progressed, and even though we felt that we had let ourselves down a bit by the performance, we did keep our record of being the only Premiership side to score in every match.

Not bad for relegation fodder!

Part of the captain's role is PR for the club and before this match I was introduced to a young Coventry fan called Matt Holland. He was a lovely kid and I hope he left the ground as happy as I did. Three points is three points is three points. As much as we want to play entertaining and exhilarating football every match, we have to remember that the currency of football is points.

1
Applauding the fans after the win away to Coventry. It was on Sky so it was a fantastic effort by those who travelled.

Saturday | 25 November 2000

Manchester City 2 v 3 Ipswich Town

MAINE ROAD: FA Carling Premier League

We viewed this as a must-win match. At the start of the season we had gone through games that were crucial six pointers and it stands to reason that the other promoted sides would definitely be those games.

We may have been flying high in the table but Burley kept reminding us that our aims from August and September remained the same, first and foremost to avoid relegation.

Manchester City were in the middle of a poor run and we compounded that by going 2-0 up in the first 32 minutes. When Stewart got his second and the team's third in the 53rd minute that should have signalled the end of the game, but with the unpredictability that makes sport so compelling, City threw everyone forward and snatched two goals back, Paulo Wanchope and Steve Howey in the 71st and 82nd minutes, respectively.

From cruising towards a secure win we were suddenly scrabbling around our own goalmouth for eight minutes as if our lives depended on it. We held on but only just and this match provided a salutary lesson. Momentum once lost is difficult to regain. I felt that at 3-0 we had become a little complacent and City had exploited that.

Burley was very complimentary to them after the match and I agreed with a lot of what he said, particularly his belief that man for man the difference between the sides was minimal but Ipswich had better continuity and confidence and that is why we were near the top and City were near the bottom.

In fact this win put us into third place. Ipswich Town - third place. What a feeling!

1
The Iceman Hreidarsson gets fiery with City's Paul Dickov.

2
'Allow me to carry you, after all I've just scored our third.'

Tuesday | 28 November 2000

Ipswich Town 2 **v** 1 Coventry City

PORTMAN ROAD: Worthington Cup 4th round

The second time we'd met in eight days and again the difference was one goal. Richard Wright was forced to miss this game after 200 consecutive appearances and I was taken off at half-time after Paul Williams had caught me late on my ankle. We were 1-0 up then thanks to Titus Bramble and his decisive end to a goalmouth scramble but Fabian conceded a penalty in the 54th minute when he brought down Chippo.

I didn't see the incident because I was getting treatment but after former Norwich player Craig Bellamy had converted it became a nerve-wracking second half. John Scales had been pushed forward into the midfield to replace me but as ever when I'm on the sidelines I kicked more times than he did. Every time one of our players got the ball I passed for him, completed the tackles and generally annoyed the people sitting next to me. It is so frustrating sitting in the stands because I live every second of the game but can do nothing to affect it.

Bad ankle or not I leapt in to the air when David Johnson cut in from the left and hit a low shot through the legs of the keeper.

All routes to Europe were still open and the good run of form, great vibes around the club and fantastic support were all continuing.

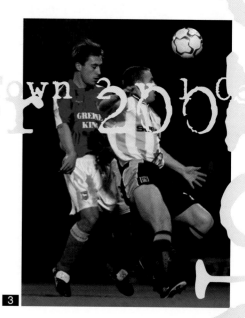

1

'Whose number one?' You are David.

2

Coventry again and Titus Bramble gives us the lead.

3

Martijn Reuser and Coventry's Barry Quinn complete for the ball.

November 2000

December 2000

December 2000

Ipswich Town 0 - 1 Derby County
Liverpool 0 - 1 Ipswich Town
Ipswich Town 3 - 1 Southampton
Manchester City 1 - 2 Ipswich Town (Worthington Cup Quarter Final)
Manchester United 2 - 0 Ipswich Town
Ipswich Town 2 - 2 Chelsea
Ipswich Town 3 - 0 Tottenham Hotspur

Saturday | 2 December 2000

Ipswich Town 0 v 1 Derby County

PORTMAN ROAD: FA Carling Premier League

The curse of awards struck as we celebrated George Burley's Manager of the Month presentation with a home defeat to one of the lesser sides in the league. Jermaine Wright gave away possession in midfield to Seth Johnson, who floated a long ball for my Republic of Ireland teammate, Rory Delap, to chase. Jermaine, keen to atone for his error chased back well to block the shot but the ball deflected wickedly off him and into the goal. Once they were in the lead they put everyone behind the ball except a solitary striker and defended like mad. If they held out it would only be their second win of the season. They were organised and difficult to break down and finished with the points. They were fighting relegation and an away win was an enormous boost to them.

At the start of the season people believed we would be playing like that, scrabbling for crucial points for survival and hanging on with every man defending desperately to protect an unexpected lead. Disappointing as it was to lose, we must put our efforts over the season into perspective and remember the way in which we were vanquished. We, on the other hand, had no need to play backs-against-the-wall football.

It was a poor loss but we had been enjoying a good run. What we needed to do now was ensure that it was nothing more than a blip and who would you pick to play next? Well, it wouldn't be Liverpool at Anfield, but having lost to one of the weaker sides, we exemplified the topsy-turvy nature of our season by going and beating one of the best in their own stadium!

The stars of tomorrow play outside Portman Road before the Derby game.

10 December 2000 Liverpool 0 v Ipswich

Sunday | 10 December 2000

Liverpool 0 v 1 Ipswich Town

ANFIELD: FA Carling Premier League

The Marcus Stewart show won us this game with one of the finest individual goals I had seen in a long time. During stoppage time in the first half he picked the ball up on the left touch line, attacked and beat the two covering defenders - Babbel and Hyppia - and slipped casually round the goalkeeper Westerveld to neatly slide the ball in.

Goals, goals, and more goals. This was his tenth of the season so far. He couldn't stop scoring and his excellent form was one of the main reasons we were doing so well, but his game is a lot more than just scoring. He isn't the biggest or the quickest striker but his work rate is phenomenal and he uses his intelligence to pull defenders out of position and create gaps for his teammates to exploit.

This was only our second victory at Anfield in 29 visits - the other was when my mate Adam Tanner had scored - and it took a wonder goal to achieve it but we had already received a major boost when they had announced their team. At 2 p.m. the team sheets were distributed round the dressing room doors and they had Emile Heskey and Steven Gerrard among the substitutes. They still had Michael Owen and Robbie Fowler up front but Heskey had been playing well and was a huge physical presence.

Just as Derby had done to us the week before, we defended like mad in the second half. The back four were superb and resolute and Richard Wright seemed 10ft tall and 5ft wide in goal. Their desperation got the better of them as they pushed Hyppia into attack from his more usual defensive role and started punting long balls into the penalty area. Easier for us to defend, we held out for our sixth away win in the Premiership and moved back into third place.

We stayed in Manchester after the match for Tuesday's Worthington Cup and again Stewart scored. It didn't count for much though as the match was abandoned after 20 minutes at 1-1 because of torrential rain. I didn't think the game should have started because it was hard to run and keep balance and almost impossible to dribble or pass. To accommodate the fixture the players' Christmas party was cancelled and the game rescheduled for 19 December.

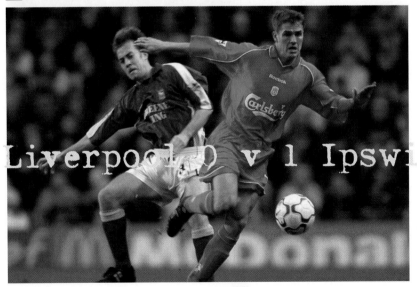

1

One of the best players in the world, Michael Owen trudges off after an unsuccessful afternoon against us.

2

You would have thought that Johnson had just scored by the celebration, but no, he and John McGreal are overjoyed to hearing the final whistle against Liverpool.

3

A bird's-eye view of Anfield.

Saturday | 16 December 2000

Ipswich Town 3 v 1 Southampton
PORTMAN ROAD: FA Carling Premier League

A slightly flattering score because we weren't two goals better than them. They were well organised and each player had a specific job to do, which they stuck to well; in other words they played like a typical Glenn Hoddle managed side. James Beattie was impressive and scored in the third minute but James Scowcroft equalised just after half-time and I felt that we had the edge over them in the important areas of the pitch and had the best chance of winning. It took Alun Armstrong on his home debut to come off the bench and score twice to ensure the victory.

A recent buy from Middlesborough, he cost £500,000 rising to £800,000 on appearances but already he was proving to be worth a lot more than that. His arrival would hopefully take a little of the pressure off Marcus Stewart and he fitted straight into the team brilliantly. We were still churning out good performances and getting the results. From a personal point of view I was very happy with my contributions. Since my early season injury I had produced a consistency of performance, as had many others and we had learned to bounce back after defeats. Our strength and resilience were carrying us on occasions, but the Premiership gives a thorough examination of a lot of attributes over the full nine months and everything has to be up to standard, so our ability to win when off-key was as satisfying as the days where we blitzed the opposition.

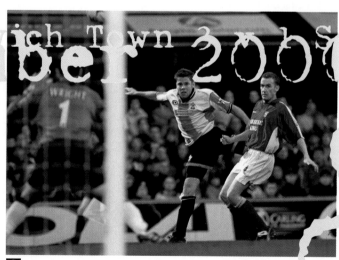

1
Presented with Manager of the Month before the Southampton match, Burley shows it off to the crowd.

2
Alun Armstrong enjoys his home debut with two goals.

3
Southampton's James Beattie goes for goal.

Tuesday | 19 December 2000

Manchester City 1 v 2 Ipswich Town

MAINE ROAD: Worthington Cup Quarter Final

Back to one leg for this stage of the competition and it couldn't have started worse for us. Mind you, it was self-inflicted. A deflected shot from Shaun Goater gave them the lead in the 10th minute and they would have gone further ahead four minutes later but the post rescued us. We had little fluency or organisation in the first half and were lucky to be only one goal down at the break.

The half-time talk helped us greatly as Burley got the white board out and showed where and how we were losing the tactical battle. Frequently, he waits for Dale Roberts or the chief scout to come down from their vantage point higher in the stand, listens to their opinions and perspectives and then works on constructing a better system for the second half. He is very analytical and very composed. He is not prone to ranting and raving for the sake of it but if he feels that we haven't put enough effort in he explodes like a volcano - and quite rightly so!

He replaced Hreidarsson with Jermaine Wright and we adopted a more traditional 4-4-2.

Burley's shrewd analysis of the situation was proved correct because we were a different unit after the break and deservedly equalised on the hour. I can't say it was a classic goal. They failed to clear a corner and Magilton's cross to Johnson was saved, but not held by Nicky Weaver and I was lethal from a yard.

I make no mistake from that distance, even with my left foot!

When the game went into extra time we felt we should win because we had finished stronger and were fitter. Mark Venus capped a fine performance by scoring the winning goal after a neat one-two with Scowcroft. It had been an exhausting night compounded by a 90-minute delay at Manchester airport because the staff had lost our luggage. Manchester City fans taking their revenge I suppose.

1

Getting the equaliser in the rearranged quarter-final against Manchester City. Even I don't miss those.

2

High stepping Gary Croft denies Paulo Wanchope and Spencer Prior.

1

MATT HOLLAND - FROM WEMBLEY TO MOSCOW - Diary of a Tractor Boy

Saturday | 23 December 2000

Manchester United 2 v 0 Ipswich Town

OLD TRAFFORD : FA Carling Premier League

With rescheduling of fixtures we felt as if we had been playing non-stop, a situation that could have been soul destroying if we had been losing. Fortunately we were on a roll but our depth of talent and strength was to be severely examined over the Christmas period. It could be nothing else with away fixtures to Manchester United and Sunderland sandwiching home fixtures against Chelsea and Tottenham, and all in the space of eight days.

Four hugely difficult matches on the trot, particularly after our exhausting lead up to Christmas. Still, this is where we wanted to be so it was up to us to prove that we deserved to be playing these matches. We didn't feel like impostors, we were in the top five of the table, but this eight-day period was the sternest possible test for the club.

And it didn't start well.

Quite frankly, Manchester United gave us a footballing lesson.

The stadium was magnificent; 67,597 fans crammed in for their biggest crowd in 67 years, and Beckham, Giggs and Co gave them a display to cherish.

Two sensational goals in the first half killed the game as we failed to defend their quick passing and movement into space. At half-time Burley tore into us for giving them too much respect, of being overawed for the first time during the season. We competed more in the second period but rarely threatened their goal and I got the feeling that they were cruising, having won the game in the first half. Apart from his excellent display on the pitch, Beckham was outstanding off it as well. He gives so much time to kids, talking to them and signing autographs, and yet regularly gets lambasted in the press. He chatted amiably as he signed two shirts for me, which I gave to the Essex and England cricketer Peter Such for his benefit year. The pressure Beckham is under is enormous though, sadly, not enough came from me during the game.

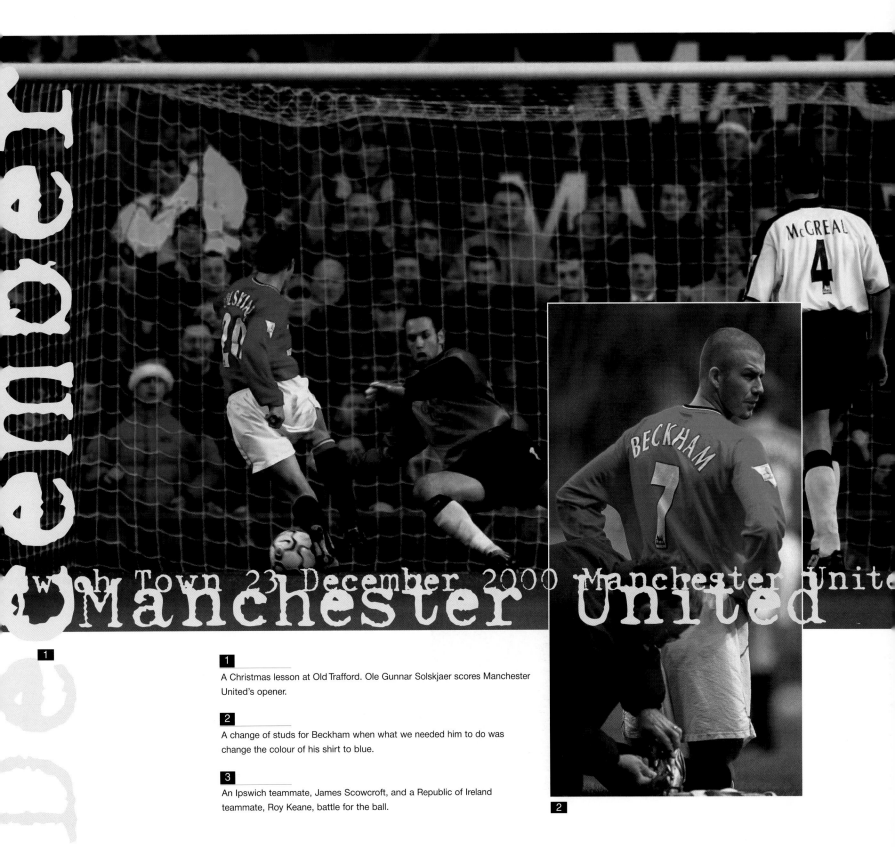

Ipswich Town 23 December 2000 Manchester United

Manchester United

1

A Christmas lesson at Old Trafford. Ole Gunnar Solskjaer scores Manchester United's opener.

2

A change of studs for Beckham when what we needed him to do was change the colour of his shirt to blue.

3

An Ipswich teammate, James Scowcroft, and a Republic of Ireland teammate, Roy Keane, battle for the ball.

Tuesday | 26 December 2000

Ipswich Town 2 v 2 Chelsea
PORTMAN ROAD: FA Carling Premier League

Normally we spend Christmas night at a hotel to ensure that we are in the correct frame of mind and properly prepared for the Boxing Day match, but this year Burley allowed everyone to stay at home with their families.

So, like all parents with two kids, I was woken Christmas morning at the crack of dawn and drowned in a sea of wrapping paper. Off to training where Mike Salmon modelled a present he had received - a leopard-print thong - and then back home for the arrival of both families. Chaos ensued, but in which house doesn't it? And for the first time in years, I experienced it all.

Again we started poorly and conceded two goals to Gudjohnsen in the first 16 minutes. He had impressed when at Bolton and was making the most of his move to Chelsea. We didn't buckle though and fought back well, probably a reaction from our insipid capitulation at Old Trafford.

Two minutes before half-time we dragged one back through Scowcroft and went into the interval psyched up that we could get something out of this game. They hadn't won an away game all season and we were determined not to be their first. We came out and played superbly, a complete contrast to the opening 20 minutes. The equaliser came in the 81st minute, another thank you to Marcus Stewart, but numerous chances could have been converted before then. A snatched victory was also possible but they defended well.

A defeat and a draw were not ideal but we had demonstrated a willingness to fight and compete.

On a personal level I was honoured to be voted the thirteenth best player in the Premiership by the football writers of the Independent newspaper. Absolutely no shock that four of the top five spots were Manchester United players (Keane, Beckham, Scholes and Sheringham) but it was heartening to know that my efforts and performances were being recognised by knowledgeable football writers with no Ipswich bias.

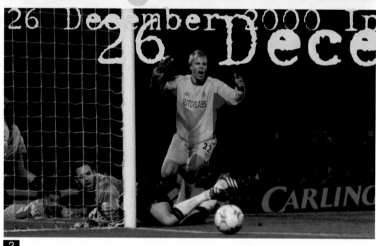

1

Out for the count on Boxing Day but Scowcroft has just scored our first goal in the comeback against Chelsea.

2

Two looks of despair and one of relief as Eidur Gudjohnsen shoots wide.

Saturday | 30 December 2000

Ipswich Town 3 v 0 Tottenham

PORTMAN ROAD: FA Carling Premier League

The win we needed and it came in some style on Sky TV.

For many football fans around the country this performance confirmed how good we were and that our elevated league position was no fluke.

Our chief assassin who had done so much to put us at the top, Stewart, started the goals in the 9th minute but we had to wait until the 66th and 88th for the other two that confirmed our dominance. Spurs were poor but we felt afterwards that our excellence had made them struggle. It was a revenge win after they had beaten us on the first day of the season and their manager George Graham was moved to apologise to the Spurs fans for the pathetic showing by his team. Their first shot came in the 57th minute, that is how dominant we were and a lot came from our control of midfield. I was given the Man of the Match but Martijn Reuser deserved it. He played up front with Armstrong and Stewart and the three of them dovetailed beautifully together.

A cracking end to the year and one that summed up the joy of the previous twelve months. Well done to the players, club and most importantly fans.

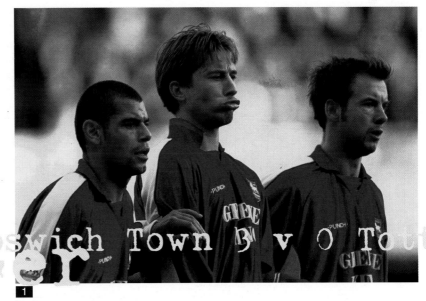

Jermaine Wright, Martijn Reuser and Marcus Stewart make a wall against Tottenham Hotspur. Reuser looks particularly nervous.

January

January 2001

Second Half

January 2001

Sunderland 4 - 1 Ipswich Town
Morecambe 0 -3 Ipswich Town FA Cup Third Round
Ipswich Town 1 - 0 Birmingham City Worthington Cup Semi Final 1st Leg
Ipswich Town 2 - 0 Leicester City
Chelsea 4 - 1 Ipswich Town
Sunderland 1 - 0 Ipswich Town FA Cup 4th Round
Birmingham City 4 - 1 Ipswich Town Worthington Cup Semi Final 2nd Leg

Monday | 1 January 2001

Sunderland 4 v 1 Ipswich Town

STADIUM OF LIGHT: FA Carling Premier League

So much for a happy new year.

We spent New Year's Eve in a hotel and I was asleep at midnight.

I actually played well next day but despite a good start, we got thumped. We changed our formation from the home victory against Spurs, trying to be more solid because it was a tricky away fixture and for once it was us that got the early goal. Sunderland play a high defensive line and I got behind it chasing a pass from Wilnis. I squared the ball and Stewart delicately chipped the keeper. A classic counter-attack strike and a super finish from the man in form.

A good free kick by Arca into the top left-hand corner made it 1-1 but at half-time we were still in the game and indeed a little aggrieved at not being in the lead.

In recent times we had dramatically improved in the second half but this game was the complete antithesis. Appaling is the best way to describe it. Two soft goals were conceded and we were out of the game. They played well and deserved to win but we just went walkabout and got exactly what our efforts warranted, a heavy defeat.

In the players' lounge after the game my dad and I spoke to Peter Reid, the Sunderland manager. He was very complimentary about Ipswich and the quality of football we had played during the season. It's always easy to be gracious when you've won but he was very sincere and very encouraging towards us. By the time we left the ground my dad had forgotten the result, Reid had been his hero and now he had met and chatted to him.

Kevin Phillips beats the off-side trap to score Sunderland's second goal.

Saturday | 6 January 2001

Morecambe 0 v 3 Ipswich Town
CHRISTIE PARK: AXA Sponsored FA Cup 3rd round

These early rounds are notorious for giant killing and however superior we appeared on paper, there was no complacency about our away trip to Morecambe. One of the fears that the bigger clubs have when they travel to lower-league or non-league opposition is the state of the pitch. A sub-standard surface often narrows the gap in skill levels between the teams, makes for a scrappy match in which passing and dribbling are more difficult and gives the lesser side a better chance.

The pitch that Morecambe provided was excellent. They wanted to watch good football and supplied a pitch for exactly that and I hope we didn't disappoint them. Jim Bowen of Bullseye certainly smiled throughout the day even though his team was losing.

The game was notable for the appearance of Richard Logan, a talented 19-year-old who made his first senior start of the season as a late replacement for Marcus Stewart. The rumours circulating the club were that the recent bid for David Johnson by Nottingham Forest would prove successful and even though Johnson was not available because of a slight groin strain, it was maybe indicative of Burley's thinking that he was keen to get Logan involved.

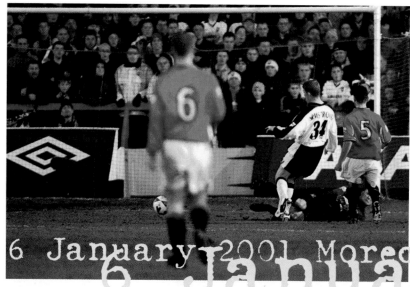

1
'You can't beat a bit of bully'. Life-long Morecambe fan and presenter of TV show Bullseye Jim Bowen watches the FA cup.

2
Alun Armstrong coolly scores our second goal and effectively ends this third-round match.

3
Rightly though, the Morecambe fans enjoyed the day, even if this was as close as both clubs got to a cup.

Tuesday | 9 January 2001

Ipswich Town 1 v 0 Birmingham City

PORTMAN ROAD: Worthington Cup Semi-final 1st Leg

This was a crucial match with the winners of the competition entering the UEFA Cup the following season and the important finance, prestige and exposure which that would bring the club. Also Ipswich had not had a major final for 23 years. The play-off final was a fantastic occasion but it wasn't the same as the defeat of Arsenal in 1978 in the FA Cup. It served a purpose rather than won a trophy.

On the way into the ground I bumped into David Platt, the then Forest manager. He was there for Johnson, the move being completed for £3 million later that week, and his assistant joked about me, 'We'll take him as well.'

'Why?' responded Platt with a huge grin. 'I can still run faster than him now.'

A penalty just before half-time was the only goal and gave us the slenderest of leads for the return leg. Ironically, it was an ex-Blues player, Danny Sonner, who handballed and Stewart calmly converted. Sonner was at the club when I first joined and his energy made him an asset in the dressing room, although sometimes we despaired. He spent weeks in the dark at home because he didn't know how to change a light bulb or that he could take one from one socket and put it in another. It certainly showed in the combination of colours he chose to wear!

With away goals counting double it was good to keep a clean sheet but we could have done with another goal and lived to regret Hreidarsson hitting a post.

1
Titus Bramble, a definite star in the making if he learns to concentrate for the whole 90 minutes.

2
Worthington Cup this time and Birmingham's Martin Connor gives referee Clive Wilkes the benefit of his opinion.

Sunday | 14 January 2001

Ipswich Town 2 v 0 Leicester City
PORTMAN ROAD: FA Carling Premier League

First game since the departure of Johnson and despite his being marginalised by other acquisitions, he had been a valuable source of goals and had been instrumental in our gaining promotion.

However, his transfer had also been good business as Burley had made a profit and balancing the books is very important for Ipswich. No one wants to return to the days of debt that David Sheepshanks had worked so hard to recover from. We were the featured TV game on Sunday and were graced with the presence of the new England manager Sven Goran Eriksson. His first weekend in the job and he comes to Ipswich!

At least we put on a show for him. It may have taken us until the 80th minute to score but we dominated from the very start. Marcus Stewart was being mentioned in dispatches for England before this game and he set to the Leicester defence like a man possessed. Of course, it was him when we finally scored although it took a sliced shot by Armstrong to find Stewart unmarked and close to goal. Still, he needed good reactions and touch to head the ball into the net and he proved to all those watching what we had known for some weeks - that he was one of the best strikers in the league and was now at the top of the goalscorers' charts with 14.

Jamie Scowcroft sealed the game in the 89th minute with a diving header and we were back in fourth place and had reached that magic number - 40 points.

Safe from relegation. Say it to yourself and think back to how good it felt at the time. We may take it for granted now because hopefully the club has moved on and won't get embroiled in that battle for many years to come, but at the time it was a special feeling for players and fans. I should know, enough of you came up to me in the days afterwards to tell me.

1

Stewart and Scowcroft celebrate another Stewart goal in front of the newly appointed England manager Sven Goran Erikkson.

2

No fingerprints were left at the scene as Leicester's Andy Impey attempts to steal the ball from Jamie Clapham.

1

Monday | 20 January 2001

Chelsea 4 v 1 Ipswich Town

STAMFORD BRIDGE: FA Carling Premier League

It is a dreadful cliché and I am loathed to use it but this really was a game of two halves, and for once we dominated the first and got hammered in the second.

Earlier in the season we had developed a habit of transforming ourselves at half-time and outplaying the opposition in the second half, exactly what Chelsea did to us in this match.

Stewart scored in the 23rd minute but annoyingly we allowed them to equalise in time added on to the first half when Richard Wright misjudged a corner and Gustavo Poyet scored. Scoring at the very end of a half gives a side a tremendous boost and momentum for the next half. Away from home we needed to defend our lead until the break and make them start panicking about getting back in the game. Instead we let them back in and they took control from that point on.

Claudio Ranieri, the Chelsea manager has long advocated the importance of a team being able to change its system, sometimes in mid-match and they did that now. From a standard 4-4-2 they moved to 3-5-2 and overran us in midfield. They did play some exceptional football but we became more and more ragged. They deserved their victory but the disappointment didn't stop with the result.

In the 73rd minute Wilnis won the ball in our penalty area but the referee, Andy D'Urso awarded a penalty. Even Poyet said after the match in the press conference that they had been given a penalty they hadn't even appealed for or considered. The game was probably beyond us at this point and they duly scored to make it 4-1 but before the kick John McGreal was sent off for foul and abusive language to D'Urso.

I was there trying to calm our player down and McGreal accused D'Urso of being a 'big time Charlie' for wanting to get in the match and give a decision to the big home club. That is why he got sent off. After the final whistle Jim Magilton carried on the protest and duly got reported for a verbal volley, a report that ensured he received a suspension.

Chelsea outplayed us but D'Urso belittled us.

Two away losses in the league with 4-1 scorelines was no preparation for the Stadium of Light and the FA Cup, particularly as Sunderland had inflicted the first of those defeats on us at the start of the month.

1
Not this time Jimmy. The ball gives me a tick for a well-executed header.

2
The man with the Golden Boot. The eventual winner of the top goalscorers award, Jimmy Floyd Hasselbaink, out jumps our defence.

3
Chelsea have the last laugh though and, here, Gustavo Poyet scores the equaliser on the stroke of half-time.

Saturday | 27 January 2001

Sunderland 1 v 0 Ipswich Town

STADIUM OF LIGHT: AXA Sponsored FA Cup 4th round

Out of the cup. This is one competition that I've never done well in and it is so disappointing because when I was a kid FA Cup final day was one of the flagship events of the sporting calendar. It was always going to be a tough match because Sunderland had not lost at home all season but we created plenty of chances, probably more than them and failed to convert a single one.

Danny Dichio's goal in the 23rd minute was enough and even though we didn't know it at the time, it started a dreadful run for the club that threatened to disrupt all the good work already done.

1
Disappointed at the defeat but your support was appreciated. I always thank the fans for they really are the club.

2
The pressure tells on the faces of the bench as Sunderland end our FA Cup dreams.

Wednesday | 31 January 2001

Birmingham City 4 v 1 Ipswich Town

ST. ANDREWS: Worthington Cup Semi-final 2nd leg

Another route to Europe closed. We had high hopes of reaching the final, not only because we felt we were a better side than Birmingham, but because we had a one-goal lead from the first leg. This was my 200th consecutive game for the club and sadly it proved to be an eminently forgettable one.

It was a physical contest. Their captain Martin O'Connor promised as much before the game, and they didn't disappoint. It was their plan to intimidate, harass and unsettle us and they did all three. Again we conceded a goal at the end of the first half and we started to look jaded as the match went on. They went 2-0 up in the 56th minute but one minute later James Scowcroft scored ... if there were no more goals in normal or extra time we would win on away goals.

When extra time started we were half an hour, just thirty minutes away from a Wembley final. Glory and Europe beckoned but they scored twice, we became ever-more tired and in the space of four days we had been knocked out of both cup competitions.

Our dressing room was absolutely silent after the match, everyone just sat there, numb as the loss sunk in.

I was so upset that I refused to do a TV interview afterwards. Normally, I make sure I am available because the media is very important but I couldn't speak. We had been so close but it counted for nothing.

1
Jamie Scowcroft celebrates his goal that is all we had to be happy about as Birmingham secured a berth at Wembley for the Worthington Cup final.

2
Ugly scenes as Birmingham fans storm the pitch. Thankfully, our supporters are better behaved.

February 2001

February 2001

Ipswich Town 1 - 2 Leeds United
Arsenal 1 - 0 Ipswich Town
Ipswich Town 2 -0 Everton

Monday | 3 February 2001

Ipswich Town 1 v 2 Leeds United

PORTMAN ROAD: FA Carling Premier League

Three consecutive defeats had dented the confidence that had been pretty much ever present around the club since September and it was important that we didn't allow an excellent season to fade away into mediocrity. We may have lost this match but at least we played well. Earlier in the season we had snatched points or results when our performance had not necessarily demanded them and this game was a reverse scenario. We played well enough to get a point at least but got nothing. Maybe the club was suffering a bit of a psychological hangover having reached our target of 40 points and safety. The problem with targets is you have to keep adjusting them as the season progresses.

Now we had to snap out of any complacency or lethargy and reset new targets for the season end. Still near the top of the table, a European spot was still possible. And what greater incentive could we have at this stage of the season than that?

Mark Venus scored an own goal in the 27th minute from a low Lee Bowyer cross and then my international teammate Robbie Keane scored his fifth in six games, similar form to our own sharpshooter Stewart. Our plans for the rest of the season were altered with 16 minutes remaining when Stewart was sent off for a late tackle on Ian Harte.

Stewart hadn't actually made contact but you would never have guessed that by Harte's reaction. He writhed around on the floor in apparent agony as if he'd been wounded by a sniper.

When the Republic of Ireland met up for the next match I did make a point of talking to Harte about it and he apologised for the play-acting but that was no consolation for Stewart. He still had a three-match ban and Ipswich still needed to find goals.

But it would be churlish to begrudge Leeds the win because they were going through a difficult time with the ongoing and very public court cases against Jonathon Woodgate and Lee Bowyer.

It was four losses out of four, however, and Arsenal at Highbury next.

Honestly, there are no easy games in this league.

'What's that for?' Nothing but still Stewart had a lonely walk off and a three-match suspension.

Robbie Keane may have scored but his gymnastic form is terrible. No straight legs, no pointed toes and absolutely no style.

Saturday | 10 February 2001

Arsenal 1 v 0 Ipswich Town
HIGHFIELD: FA Carling Premier League

Thierry Henry came off the bench and scored the winner in the 58th minute. What a player to have on the bench and he had been sitting next to Dennis Bergkamp!

We could have salvaged a draw for our efforts but our star performer was undoubtedly Richard Wright.

After the game I said to the press,'That's as good a performance as I've seen from a keeper for a long time.'

Arsene Wenger was obviously impressed because he bought him in the summer.

After the match I jumped on the local Tube line to get to a train station near the M25, from where I was getting picked up to go to Bournemouth for the weekend. Resplendent in my Ipswich suit, I stood among the Ipswich and Arsenal fans and took a fair bit of gloating banter from the Gooners. It was all very good-natured and very, very funny and I quite enjoyed the journey. We now had two weeks off and we needed them. Our form had slumped and we were in danger of ruining an excellent season.

1

Ray Parlour and I tussle for the ball.

2

A sombre moment before the start as we observe a one-minute silence in memory of Arsenal youth player Niccolo Galli, 17, who died in a car crash in Italy.

3

Another great save by Richard Wright. Undoubtedly he was the star of this game.

4

You can't win them all.

Saturday | 24 February 2001

Ipswich Town 2 v 0 Everton

PORTMAN ROAD: FA Carling Premier League

After five consecutive defeats it felt great to get a win. The relief in the dressing room was almost tangible and I am convinced that it was because we were fresh in both body and mind.

The goals, by me and Alun Armstrong may have come late in the game (82nd and 84th) but we had been the more likely scorers throughout. Admittedly, the sending off of Alex Nyarko helped, the final 19 minutes becoming more like an attack-against-defence training session.

Mark Burchill, on loan from Celtic, made his debut for us in place of the suspended Stewart and played surprisingly well considering he had only spent two or three days with us. In fact both goals came from his crosses. Mine came as his cross was headed clear, bounced awkwardly in front of me, hit me in the face and then connected with my swinging left foot. Rest assured, the rest of the team took no time in reminding me that I normally only use my left foot for standing on.

Hopes of a European spot were revived and it proved to us that we could score and win without Stewart.

Denmark was my next port of call for an international friendly but it was called off due to snow. We had gone in to the cinema Monday evening with the ground clear and come out two hours later to inches of snow, inches that increased throughout Tuesday so that the game was cancelled early Wednesday morning. To compound the wasted journey we then struggled to get a flight out.

Nabil Abidallah tries to catch me after I've scored against Everton.

On loan from Celtic, Mark Burchill shoots for goal.

March

march 2001
March 2001

Ipswich Town 3 - 1 Bradford
Aston Villa 2 - 1 Ipswich Town
West Ham 0 - 1 Ipswich Town
Cyprus 0 - 4 Republic of Ireland
Andorra 0 - 3 Republic of Ireland

Sunday | 4 March 2001

Ipswich Town 3 v 1 Bradford City

PORTMAN ROAD: FA Carling Premier League

Martijn Reuser certainly showed the viewers on Sky what a skilful player he is. The two goals he scored made the Match of the Day Goal of the Month competition and helped put us back into third place, that crucial final Champions League spot.

The game didn't start that well though as we went behind to a Benito Carbone free kick, another that featured in Goal of the Month. Then it was over to Reuser. He is a very creative player and a real asset in attack, but he has imitations defensively.

That two-week break had really come at the right time for us and we started to buzz again as we contemplated the run-in and Europe. Hreidarsson must have been fresh because he jumped into Row Z of the crowd to celebrate his headed goal. Meanwhile the rest of us calmly congratulated Mark Burchill who had actually administered the final touch. Never mind, Hermann!

———— 1
In fantastic form, Martijn Reuser gives thanks for another goal.

———— 2
Hreidarsson heads for goal and it deflects in off Burchill.

———— 3
But Hreidarsson believes it's his goal and heads for the top of the stand.

Saturday | 10 March 2001

Aston Villa 2 v 1 Ipswich Town
VILLA PARK: FA Carling Premier League

The only side to do the double over us and both times 2-1. This was a poor performance and a poor game but we should have done better considering we had taken the lead through Alun Armstrong after half an hour. Chris Makin made his debut for us and ironically his final opponents for Sunderland five days earlier had been Villa.

After the game, Burley blamed two mistakes by centre halves John McGreal and Hreidarsson for their goals, although Julian Joachim did finish both well and proved how threatening his speed is.

1
Villa's David Ginola is challenged by Ipswich's Martijn Reuser.

2
Aston Villa and England keeper David James is beaten by Alun Armstrong.

3
Julian Joachim using his speed to get past Jermaine Wright.

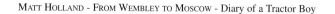

Monday | 17 March 2001

West Ham 0 v 1 Ipswich Town

UPTON PARK: FA Carling Premier League

The return of Marcus Stewart after his ban and a return to Upton Park for me. I had captained the Hammers youth team and Tony Gale, a former player and centre half, wrote some really complimentary things about me in the match programme.

Reuser was the man again, a superb free kick from just outside the penalty area in the 59th minute winning the match. Moments earlier we had felt aggrieved as Stuart Pearce had tripped Stewart in the area and we wanted the penalty but the skill of Reuser made our protests redundant. There was a very good atmosphere in the dressing room afterwards because this was our first away win - let alone points - in three months.

I flew to sunny Cyprus for a World Cup qualifier and while I was away the East Anglian Daily Times published their poll of the top 100 Ipswich players as voted by the readers.

I was the highest ranked current player at eleventh, two places higher than Richard Wright but one below the manager, George Burley, who must have received some votes for his management. That's what I told him anyway.

It was a great honour to be voted so highly and added to the good feelings I had from winning the Greene King Player of the Month awards for January and February. I received a glass tankard for each month and a bottle of Chateau Talbot red wine from 1974, the year of my birth. So many accolades, I must have been doing something right!

Shadowed by Svetoslav Todorov, I look to pass the ball.

Well held, sir. Richard Wright claims a cross against my old club West Ham United.

A stunning free kick by Reuser won the game. See how much swerve he put on the ball.

Saturday | 24 March 2001

Cyprus 0 v 4 Republic of Ireland

FIFA World Cup European Qualifying Group 2

Ah sunshine! I'd nearly forgotten what it felt like to run around and have the sun on my back.

This was a relatively simple win and I only came on as substitute in the 78th minute and as a jinking right winger at that. True to form I failed to beat a single defender but hassled and closed down my left back every time he got the ball. Old habits die hard I suppose. From Cyprus we moved to Andorra for the next qualifier and another victory.

1

Roy Keane celebrates scoring the 4th goal.

2

A familiar sight, Roy Keane dominating the opposition, this time for the Republic of Ireland against Cyprus.

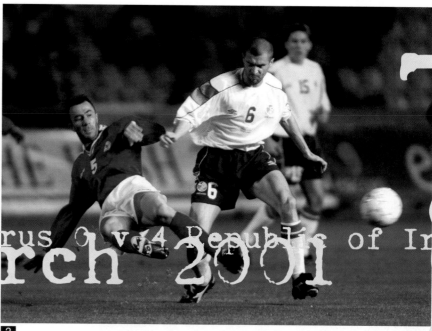

Wednesday | 28 March 2001

Andorra 0 v 3 Republic of Ireland

FIFA World Cup European Qualifying Group 2

At least this time I started and featured properly. We played at the mini Nou Camp, where Barcelona reserves play. This was a decent stadium but the day before we had toured around the Nou Camp itself, and that really is something special. From the outside it looks quite disappointing and small but that is an illusion because the actual pitch and stadium are sunk 40 feet into the ground, so outside ground level is about halfway up the stands.

Neither this performance, nor Cyprus was particularly special, more 'job done' than anything else but I did get another goal for my country. The press were a little harsh about the matches but we did enough. You want to keep your best games for the best opposition, and in this group that meant Portugal and Holland.

1

The team photo before the Andorra game. I'm smiling so I must be playing.

1

The East Anglian Daily Times Top 100 Players.

1 Kevin Beattie
2 John Wark
3 Arnold Muhren
4 Mick Mills
5 Frans Thijssen
6 Paul Mariner
7 Terry Butcher
8 Ray Crawford
9 Allan Hunter
10 George Burley
11 Matt Holland
12 Ted Phillips
13 Richard Wright
14 Billy Baxter
15 Kieron Dyer
16 Alan Brazil
17 Paul Cooper
18 Marcus Stewart
19 Mick Stockwell
20 Trevor Whymark
21 Clive Woods
22 Eric Gates
23 Mauricio Taricco
24 Colin Viljoen
25 John Elsworthy
26 Russell Osman
27 Brian Talbot
28 Jason Dozzell

29 Titus Bramble
30 Jimmy Leadbetter
31 James Scowcroft
32 Alex Mathie
33 Danny Hegan
34 Roger Osborne
35 Tony Mowbray
36 Martijn Reuser
37 Jim Magilton
38 Jimmy Robertson
39 David Linighan
40 David Johnson (1990s)
41 Chris Kiwomya
42 Jamie Clapham
43 Roy Bailey
44 Hermann Hreidarsson
45 Simon Milton
46 Romeo Zondervan
47 Craig Forrest
48 Bobby Petta
49 Tommy Parker
50 David Johnson (1970s)
51 Frank Brogan
52 Kevin Wilson
53 Jimmy McLuckie
54 Andy Nelson
55 Dalian Atkinson
56 Bontcho Guentchev

57 Ian Marshall
58 Billy Reed
59 David Geddis
60 Fabian Wilnis
61 Geraint Williams
62 Richard Naylor
63 Steve McCall
64 Neil Thompson
65 Gavin Johnson
66 Mark Venus
67 Steve Whitton
68 Tom Garneys
69 Bryan Hamilton
70 Danny Sonner
71 Alun Armstrong
72 Trevor Putney
73 Peter Morris
74 Mick Burns
75 Derek Jefferson
76 Mich D'Avray
77 Jason Cundy
78 Sergei Baltacha
79 Glenn Pennyfather
80 Paul Mason
81 Colin Harper
82 David Best
83 Dai Rees
84 Kenny Malcolm

85 Steve Sedgley
86 Joe Broadfoot
87 John McGreal
88 Frank Yallop
89 John O'Rourke
90 Laurie Sivell
91 Gus Uhlenbeek
92 Jackie Little
93 David Gregory
94 Paul Goddard
95 Ian Cranson
96 Doug Moran
97 Mick Lambert
98 Rod Belfitt
99 Jermaine Wright
100 Les Tibbott

Reproduced by courtesy of The East Anglian Daily Times.

April 2001

Southampton 0 - 3 Ipswich Town
Ipswich Town 1 - 1 Liverpool
Ipswich Town 1 - 0 Newcastle United
Middlesborough 1 - 2 Ipswich Town
Ipswich Town 2 - 0 Coventry City
Republic of Ireland 3 - 1 Andorra
Charlton Athletic 2 - 1 Ipswich Town

Monday | 2 April 2001

Southampton 0 v 3 Ipswich Town

THE DELL: FA Carling Premier League

This was the perfect time to play the Saints as the uncertainty around the club had escalated with the confirmation that Glenn Hoddle had gone to Tottenham Hotspur.

Stuart Gray, the caretaker boss, was immediately under pressure, not least because of the rumours that Hoddle wanted to take the key members of the Saints with him to White Hart Lane.

The animosity towards the former England manager was obvious. The fans felt betrayed and made their feelings known with numerous banners, placards and chants.

The effect that such an acrimonious departure can have on a club is perfectly exemplified by the swift turnround in Southampton's fortunes. Before playing us they had not conceded a single Premiership goal, nor lost since Liverpool on New Year's Day. Before Hoddle left, their consistent performances had given them hopes of Europe.

We, in the form of a Marcus Stewart hat-trick, thumped them. Sven Goran Erikkson was in the crowd and must have been impressed by our football. The first goal was indicative of the high-quality football we were playing again after our February slump.

Jamie Clapham overlapped on the left wing and the ball was worked to him. His pinpoint accurate and low cross was headed into the net by the unmarked Stewart. On TV it looked so simple and that proves how good it was. Although Stewart finished with a hat-trick, he could have had more. We created so many chances and Reuser was a constant threat, running at the hesitant Saints' defence and releasing Stewart with clever passes.

The final goal was sheer impudent cheek by Stewart but his confidence was sky-high. I had been fouled in the area by El Khalej and from the ensuing penalty, Stewart chipped the sprawling keeper and became the first player at the club to score 20 goals in a season for 18 years. A wonderful achievement but no less than he deserved for his tireless running and hard work throughout the season. Another game or two like this and he could win the coveted Golden Boot.

There was a special intensity about the club again. Europe loomed, we were back playing the excellent passing football that had won us so many neutral admirers at the start of the season and we were enjoying it again. The mid-season slump was a distant memory now.

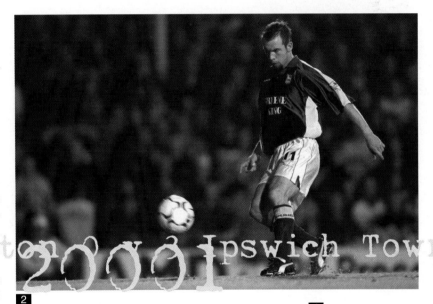

Angry Southampton fans advertise for a new manager after the acrimonious departure of Glenn Hoddle.

A cheeky chipped penalty and Stewart had his hat-trick and 20 goals for the season. Wonderful, absolutely wonderful.

10 April 2001 Ipswich Town 1 v 0 Liverpool

Tuesday | 10 April 2001

Ipswich Town 1 v 1 Liverpool

PORTMAN ROAD: FA Carling Premier League

On the Saturday (7 April) Marcus and I were featured guests on BBC's Alive and Kicking show. I took the whole family, Paula, Samuel and Jacob to watch and the children loved it because H and Clare from Steps were on the show as well. It was a fun day and Mark Lawrenson, another guest, was incredibly funny. He is a really decent guy and has a dry sense of humour. Now when I watch him on TV I laugh a lot more because I can see when he's joking.

We were surprised with Liverpool's tactics because they played only one up front - Emile Heskey - and put everybody else behind the ball. We'd expected a club that was pursuing trophies on three fronts, as well as one of two remaining and much-coveted Champions League spots, to be more dynamic and pro-active.

Admittedly, they did have a backlog of fixtures and Gerard Houllier was unhappy that this match hadn't been postponed, but we thought they would be more aggressive despite the effects of fatigue from three games in six days.

This was a double-pointer match. Manchester United had won the league to all intents and purposes but Arsenal were second (57 points), us third (52), Leeds fourth (50) and Liverpool fifth (49). All had seven games remaining except Liverpool who had nine.

A win would put us in prime position for the Champions League but with only 15 seconds of the second half gone, Chris Makin dithered over the ball and Heskey sped past, took it on to the goal and scored. It was a dreadful start to the half, compounded by Liverpool immediately becoming even more defensive in trying to protect their lead. Igor Biscan and Steven Gerrard patrolled right in front of the back four and we hurled everything and everyone forward in a desperate search for the equaliser.

Bramble and Wright were replaced by the more attacking Scowcroft and Wilnis and in the 77th minute, Armstrong sneaked round the back of the defence and side-footed a volley home from a deep cross.

A vital score and to be honest, a deserved one and it put us into third place and gave us 53 points, a tally that meant the most successful year for the club in the Premiership. Our biggest home crowd of the season were definitely pleased as 23,504 voices cheered us for our efforts.

Lone striker he may have been but Emile Heskey finished coolly to give Liverpool the lead.

Saturday | 14 April 2001

Ipswich Town 1 v 0 Newcastle United
PORTMAN ROAD: FA Carling Premier League

The return of Bobby Robson and what a reception he received. It was tremendous to hear the cheers and chants as he led Newcastle out and proved the depth of affection Ipswich still has for their former manager.

Kieron Dyer, another former favourite didn't feature though and no doubt that benefited us, as did the disallowing of a Carl Cort goal in the first half for a push. The game turned in the 76th minute when Solano handled on the line and was sent off. Stewart scored the penalty and in the last 15 minutes we could have scored more but for a series of superb saves by their keeper Shay Given. He certainly looked on great form for our World Cup qualifier against Andorra at the end of the month.

Every game was absolutely vital now and I was secretly starting to think that we could sneak into the Champions League. We were above Leeds in third place but only by goal difference. The race was on and it was that close.

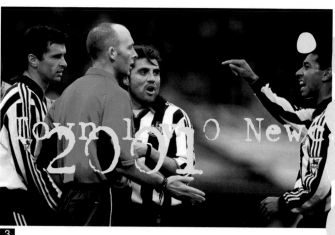

1

Like his team, George Burley was in sharper focus than his opponent, the legendary Bobby Robson.

2

HANDBALL!

3

Nolberto Solano asking the way to the dressing room having been sent off.

Monday | 16 April 2001

Middlesborough 1 v 2 Ipswich Town

RIVERSIDE STADIUM: FA Carling Premier League

This was the dream return to the Riverside for Alun Armstrong. We had flown up after the Newcastle game in high spirits and confident although we were aware that this was likely to be a tough game as Middlesborough had just beaten Arsenal at Highbury 3-0.

They were still in the relegation battle so there would be no lack of effort from them and part of the reason for their perilous position was their poor home form - they hadn't won at home since January. Their difficulties were compounded by both Coventry and Derby winning as they lost to us.

They did start quite brightly and far more organised than the corresponding fixture earlier in the season, no doubt the influence of Terry Venables, and the crowd went wild when Dean Windass gave them the lead in the 39th minute.

At half-time we changed to 4-4-2 as Clapham came on for Reuser. Within six minutes we were in the lead, both coming from Armstrong and both good goals. The first was a 20-yard strike into the left-bottom corner and the second was a wonderful predatory flick from a man in form. Stewart crossed from the left and not only did Armstrong muscle himself in front of the defender but he deftly teased the ball into the far corner across the stranded keeper. A difficult chance that needed a fine touch.

After the game everyone was buzzing for him because he was so obviously pleased to return to his former club and home and play so well. He is a great character for us and really fits in well in the dressing room. Not even his nickname of Trigger - the stupid one from Only Fools and Horses - upsets him because he is just as prepared to laugh at himself as he is at others.

Europe beckoned, we just didn't know in which format and if we continued winning it could easily be the most prestigious club competition in the world - the Champions League.

1
He saved them in the end but the pressure is starting to tell on Middlesbrough's emergency coach Terry Venables

2
And this is why. Alun Armstrong celebrates a dramatic return to the Riverside.

Saturday | 21 April 2001

Ipswich Town 2 v 0 Coventry City
PORTMAN ROAD: FA Carling Premier League

Back in August, this, and the next match against Charlton Athletic, had been earmarked as relegation clashes with the losers probably slipping back down to Division One. Instead we were challenging for Europe, Charlton were in upper mid-table and only the perennial escapologists, Coventry, were struggling.

It wasn't hard to see why after this game because we were quicker, sharper and slicker throughout, so much so that in Ireland the following week Gary Breen asked me what training we had done to make us so much quicker.

The win virtually guaranteed us a UEFA Cup spot, proof of how we had turned ourselves around after the winter.

Reuser and Wright scored the goals in the 23rd and 61st minutes, respectively. Wright's being his first goal at Portman Road and what a lovely strike it was as well. Not only that but he made Reuser's by a great run down the right and an excellent cross that myself and a defender slid for, missed and Reuser finished. In the dressing room I obviously claimed my miss was deliberate but no one believed me.

1

Faster, sharper, smarter. Hreidarsson jumps a clumsy challenge by Coventry's Marc Edworthy.

2

Coventry City manager Gordon Strachan didn't quite make it though as his side were relegated and he lost his job.

Wednesday | 25 April 2001

Republic of Ireland 3 v 1 Andorra

FIFA World Cup European Qualifying Group 2

I started and played a full game and afterwards we went back top of the group. What was billed as an easy fixture started badly as they took the lead in the 31st minute, but possibly shaken from our lethargy we struck back twice within five minutes to take a lead. Having been galvanised into action by their goal we passed and linked well but found their eleven-man defence difficult to break down. Gary Breen managed it in the 73rd minute and that effectively was the match won. We were still unbeaten, had 14 points and were top of the group, not bad considering the quality of the group but we knew the next three games were the make or break ones.

1

Gary Breen wraps it up for the Republic with our third goal.

2

The match-specific shirts hang proudly in my wardrobe at home. This one clearly shows it was against Andorra.

30 April 2001 Charlton Athletic 2 v 1 Ipswich
30 April 2001

Monday | 30 April 2001

Charlton Athletic 2 v 1 Ipswich Town

THE VALLEY: FA Carling Premier League

The encouraging aspect of this match was that both sides were supposed to be relegation fodder and yet had survived, if not excelled by adhering to the simple ideas of good, passing football. This book is about Ipswich but much that has been written about style, hunger and passion could equally apply to Charlton and they proved it by inflicting the first defeat upon us in front of the Sky cameras. The game itself was decent and pretty even despite us having more chances and they proved their adaptability by altering to a 4-3-3 formation for the second half from a three-man defence. Martijn Reuser continued his scintillating form by nullifying Mattias Svensson's opener in the 21st minute, although it was a little fortuitous that everyone including the keeper missed his cross and watched it creep in the far corner of the goal.

Richard Rufus won it for them though in the 56th minute, taking full advantage of a poorly defended free kick. After that we threw men forward but to no avail. We remained in fourth place despite the defeat and Charlton moved up to eighth, a very creditable effort.

1

Superb to play alongside, Jim Magilton blocks Charlton's Mark Kinsella.

2

A perfectly timed tackle against Charlton Athletic and as usual my left foot is good for nothing.

may 2001
May 2001

Ipswich Town 2 - 1 Manchester City
Derby County 1 - 1 Ipswich Town

Monday | 7 May 2001

Ipswich Town 2 v 1 Manchester City

PORTMAN ROAD: FA Carling Premier League

Our last home game of the season and we were honoured with another record crowd - 25,004. It was always likely to be an exciting game as both sides desperately needed to win. We needed to keep alive our slim hopes of qualifying for the Champions League and they wanted to avoid relegation.

Before the game, their manager Joe Royle said that if Ipswich had not been promoted via the play-offs the season before he would have tried to buy me. And now we beat them, I scored and it confirmed that they were going down. How ironic.

As you would expect they fought like dervishes and took the lead in the 74th minute through Shaun Goater. At this stage and scoreline they could still stay up but four minutes later I was in my usual lurking position on the edge of their penalty box. I latched on to a knock down and rifled it home for the equaliser. It got worse for them as they discarded caution and went for the win with three strikers leaving us vast space in which to develop attacks. In the 85th minute they suffered as Reuser was unmarked and successfully completed a diving header from an Armstrong cross. Thank goodness we won the final home match of the season because the support had been fantastic all year. We did a lap of honour to thank the fans because we realise that without the support we, ourselves, would be nothing.

I always go to all parts of a ground to thank fans anyway because I appreciate that many will have spent a lot of time and money travelling to watch, just as I did when I was younger with my dad.

I felt a little sorry for Royle, the City players and fans because they had had such high hopes when they had won promotion the year before, but from a selfish point of view it kept us in the mix for that final Champions League place. What a dream that would be. Division One to Champions League in 12 months.

The day after the match the North Stand demolition started and the players decamped to Magaluf for a quick break. Golf was the favourite activity and a few of us went to watch Real Mallorca v Celta Vigo. Just sampling the kind of stuff we could expect next season, you see.

1

And like Gordon Strachan of Coventry, Joe Royle was sacked as manager.

2

Relegation hurts. Manchester City's Steve Howey is distraught after defeat to us put them down.

19 May 2001 Derby County 1 v 1 Ipswich

Saturday | 19 May 2001

Derby County 1 v 1 Ipswich Town

PRIDE PARK STADIUM: FA Carling Premier League

The final day of the season and I felt absolutely awful. I had the flu and as hard as I tried during the game I just couldn't muster up the necessary energy to have a great impact. In fact, I felt exhausted. The story before the start was that we needed to win and we needed both Leeds United and Liverpool to lose for us to sneak into third place, but they both won comfortably, rendering our match meaningless, which was a fair reflection of a totally forgettable game. It was a great effort by the 4,000 Blues fans who travelled there and the fancy dress costumes were certainly eye-catching, at least I hope they were fancy dress!

The support away from home had been excellent all season and I'd like to thank you all on behalf of everybody at the club. The players definitely appreciate it.

At the time we did not realise that it would be Richard Wright's last game and I know the whole club was sad to see such a high-quality keeper leave. His huge presence between the posts had been an instrumental factor in our success and I'm sure that he will prove an excellent acquisition for Arsenal.

I must also mention the exceptional season enjoyed by Marcus Stewart. He was replaced by Richard Naylor in the 40th minute of this match due to an injury he picked up. I believe he is one of the unluckiest footballers around to not get called up for international duty. Sadly, he also just missed out on the Golden Boot - Jimmy Floyd Hasselbaink of Chelsea won it - but none of that can ever detract from his phenomenal season and he deservedly won our Player of the Year award. To think we had only bought him midway through the previous season. What a shrewd buy that was by the manager.

1 Rueing a missed chance. At this stage we didn't know our match was irrelevant.

2 Almost worth an invite to the end-of-season party.

3 The end of the league at Derby and a final farewell from Richard Wright, although we didn't know that then.

4 George Burley was voted as Carling Manager of the Year. Thoroughly deserved award after our tremendous season.

June

June 2001

June 2001

Republic of Ireland 1 - 1 Portugal
Estonia 0 - 2 Republic of Ireland

Saturday | 2 June 2001

Republic of Ireland 1 v 1 Portugal

FIFA World Cup European Qualifying Group 2

It had been a long and exhausting season, as well as an exhilarating one, but it wasn't over just yet. As other players jetted off on well-deserved holidays, Hermann Hreidarsson and I joined our respective national teams for the final World Cup qualifier games of the season.

First we had the vital match against one of the group favourites, Portugal, and it was imperative we got a point at the very least. Steve Staunton won his 88th cap and equalled the record of Tony Cascarino, and Roy Keane, as ever, was absolutely fantastic. Without him we would have been blown away in the first half. Portugal were at their sumptuous best, skilful, instinctive and dominant and I felt that we were lucky to be 0-0 at half-time. A lot of that was thanks to Shay Given in goal. He had excelled for Newcastle against Ipswich only a couple of months earlier and if anything this was an even better performance.

I was on the bench and frustrated but the second half was more equal as the wind picked up. In fact, for periods of it we managed to get on top of them and Roy Keane scored in the 65th minute. Ten minutes later Niall Quinn was taken off and I went on to play directly in front of the back four. Our intent was obvious. A striker had come off and we were defending with everything to try and protect our lead and a crucial three points. We couldn't hold out as they threw more men forward and attacked almost constantly for the last 15 minutes. In the 80th minute a long cross found Luis Figo at the back post and he headed in. From then on the game kind of fizzled out and disappointing as it was to let in an equaliser, if someone had offered us a draw at half-time we would probably have taken it.

However, the animosity that had started when one of their representatives complained about the training facilities continued at the end of the game as their manager Antonio Oliveria refused to shake Mick McCarthy's hand. Real handbags at six paces stuff!

The other event was the booking of Roy Keane, so I knew I would be playing against Estonia as he served his suspension.

1
Luis Figo of Portugal scoring and celebrating his crucial equaliser. At the time he was the world's most expensive player at over £45 million.

2
And a man who probably would have been in his era. One of the world's greatest ever footballers at Lansdowne Road for the match, Portugal's Eusebio.

Wednesday | 6 June 2001

Estonia 0 v 2 Republic of Ireland

FIFA World Cup European Qualifying Group 2

The other Keane, Robbie, also missed out but his was selectorial whim rather than discipline, Damien Duff replacing him up front.

Before the match, McCarthy had reminded us that this was no pushover. Estonia had recently led Holland 2-1 only to concede three goals in the last 10 minutes.

Richard Dunne gave us the perfect start with a goal in the 8th minute and this settled the team into a good rhythm of possession. At the start we were a little taken aback by the poor quality of the pitch as the ball bobbled everywhere, making passing and control more difficult. Mind you, maybe it was a bobble that made me connect so well with my shot from the edge of the box that made it 2-0. If the ball had rolled smoothly towards me I 'd probably have shinned it to the corner flag.

Never were we under threat in the match and afterwards there was a sense of satisfaction at a job well done. We hugged and congratulated each other, pleased at the result and also a little demob happy as the season was now over. I was elated at the way the season had gone, both for club and country and keen to get home, collect Paula and the two boys and head off for a welcome holiday in Marbella, Spain.

Ole!

Pre-Season

No sooner had it finished, than it started again and I was pleased. I love football and although I know the importance, and enjoy a break, I start to get itchy feet and excited about playing again. Six weeks after I headed off to Spain, I was back at Portman Road and off to Estonia and Finland for a pre-season tour.

Richard Wright was gone, Jamie Scowcroft was going and Finidi George was on his way. The changes had been minimal at Ipswich but we did discover a new supporter. While in Tallinn in Estonia we were introduced to Elton John backstage before a concert. A famous football fan, he congratulated us on our success and spoke very knowledgeably to me about our style, the changes in the game and the forthcoming World Cup games. He certainly knew his stuff. The squad then joined the audience to watch his show, which as you'd expect was brilliant and even more so because he mentioned Ipswich Town and dedicated a song to us - 'I guess that's why they call them the Blues'.

Because this book was meant to feature one season alone, I will not start discussing any club matches in the 2001/2 season but I will indulge myself by finishing with the crucial World Cup qualifier at Lansdowne Road against Holland.

We needed a point, the three we got effectively ensured us the play-off position and a match against the third best Asian side. Win that and we'd go to the 2002 World Cup in Japan and Korea.

That is why this 1-0 win with only ten men for nearly 30 minutes of the match was such a famous victory.

Saturday | 1 September 2001

Republic of Ireland 1 v 0 Holland

FIFA World Cup European Qualifying Group 2

1

The win against Holland was a fantastic achievement and Shay Given deserves every bit of applause he received for keeping superbly.

2

Never far from Patrick Kluivert, I defend our one-goal lead. Ruud van Nistlerooy's shirt hangs proudly at home as a special reminder of a great day.

The game that knocked one of the best sides in the world out of the World Cup, and gave us a superb chance of being in it. The feeling around Lansdowne Road and Dublin after the match was electric and I ended up in a bar singing Irish songs while trying to watch Germany - England on the TV.

First let me bathe in the glory of the Republic's win.

Holland had thumped England only a few weeks before, albeit in a friendly and had demonstrated why they are considered to be one of the best teams to watch in world football. However, we needed a result and at the risk of sounding boring or repeating myself, Roy Keane was absolutely extraordinary. Whatever talent they had, and in Van Bommel, Cocu, Zenden, Kluivert and company, they certainly had plenty, Keane stood out. He covered every blade of grass, several times, in snuffing out the Dutch attacks and when Gary Kelly was sent off, Keane exhorted the rest of us to work harder and set about single-handedly making up for the numerical discrepancy.

The goal came as a shock and again the initial impetus came from Keane on the left, but it was an exquisite chip by Steve Finnan and clinical finish by Jason McAteer that sent the fans wild.

The final 20 minutes were real backs-to-the-wall stuff and I tried to surgically attach myself to Kluivert. We held on and showed the spirit and resilience that had left us unbeaten throughout the qualifying group stage.

Having rescued Bryan from Westlife from my drunken brother I found the pre-arranged bar where my wife and friends were, clutched a pint of the black stuff, cleared my throat for a few arias of 'Come on you boys in green' and marvelled at England destroying their footballing nemesis - Germany.

Of that game there is little to say. Gerrard, Beckham and, of course, Owen were superb and the Germans surprisingly poor but it did re-ignite the hopes that both England and the Republic of Ireland would be at the finals. Who says our football is struggling?

olland 1 September 2001 Republic of Ireland 1
September 2001
IRELAND V HOLLAND
IRELAND

Conclusion

No doubt you will remember some of the incidents and events during these games differently, but these are my memories from down on the pitch and, if I was doing my job right, in the thick of the action.

It was an extraordinary season. Undoubtedly we were lucky. We suffered few injuries and the depth of our squad was not severely examined, but in mitigation we are not a dirty side. Our disciplinary record was one of the best and that is because we concentrated on good discipline and good football. Which is proved by us winning the Premier League Fair Play Table.

There is little petulance or ego in Ipswich Town. There is a job to do and that is to win matches. Posturing and posing hold little interest for us. Hard work, both individually and collectively were the cornerstones of our success and it started with the management team and George Burley.

Quite how we challenged for a Champions League place, however, I do not know. Yes we played well, but I think the rest underestimated us and treated us as relegation fodder and suffered as a consequence. The hard part will be to try and to maintain the standards we set this season. It will not be easy but we have to try and develop a long-term residency in the top league and hope for European ventures. The thing we must avoid is relegation. All the good work we have done will be lost if we slip back into Division One, so disappointing as it may be, fourth from bottom will still be a creditable performance. Not good, we understand that, but we also realise that survival is still everything. I just hope we can keep surviving near the top of the table!

My final words go to the players. The dressing room was a fun and enjoyable place to be during the season, winning does that to camaraderie and confidence, and I know that we enjoyed the season immensely. Hope you did, too.

Matt Holland